THE ROOTS OF
BLACK POVERTY

To Those Who Are Dear To Me
Joan and Jonny
Bub and Poppy

THE ROOTS OF BLACK POVERTY

THE SOUTHERN PLANTATION ECONOMY
AFTER THE CIVIL WAR

Jay R. Mandle

DUKE UNIVERSITY PRESS   DURHAM, N.C.   1978

© 1978, Duke University Press

L.C.C. card no. 78-52026

I.S.B.N. 0-8223-0408-2

080990

Printed in the United States of America

PREFACE

The historical roots of contemporary black poverty constitute the central focus of this study. The basic problem which is analyzed is why incomes received by blacks in the decades after the Civil War and Emancipation remained disproportionately low compared to incomes received by other groups in American society. To provide an answer to this question requires, in turn, an analysis of both the causes and consequences of the fact that the black population remained predominantly southern as late as the years of World War II and its aftermath. A third issue which is considered is the southern blacks' response to this situation and the strategies which they adopted to overcome that poverty. The book concludes with a brief assessment of current prospects for overcoming black poverty.

Although the post-bellum South is increasingly the object of scholarly attention, these questions have largely been overlooked. In recent years several economic historians have contributed analyses of the performance of the southern economy after the Civil War and have given particular attention to the black experience in that economy. Much attention, for example, has been devoted to the economic consequences of share tenancy as an important organizational form in southern agriculture. These efforts, however, tend to focus on the classic economic problems of resource allocation and market efficiency. They do so at the expense of a systematic investigation of the ultimate source of black poverty: the underdeveloped nature of the economy of those parts of the South in which the black population was concentrated.

To address this neglected subject the Marxian concept of a mode of production is employed. The limited economic development experienced in the South, it is argued, was the result of plantation dominance. Furthermore, salient features of the plantation mode of production were repression and enforced immobility. These restrictions both prevented blacks from moving to other regions and were central to the limited economic development experienced in the region.

I first formulated the model of the plantation economy and argued that this mode of production was distinct from a capitalist mode in exploring the reasons for the lack of economic development in Guyana, formerly the colony of British Guiana.[1] Throughout the writing of that analysis the question of the similarity between the Guyanese experience and that of other parts of the New World was a recurring issue. At the time, however, I was not able to explore fully this dimension of the problem. Other Caribbeanists, however, are aware of the comparable patterns of development which were experienced in those parts of the New World where plantations came to dominate the economy. Thus, as an example, George F. Beckford in his recent discussion of third world plantation economics makes repeated references to the United States South.[2] Following the lead of Beckford and other scholars, I treat the post-bellum South as essentially different from the rest of the United States and possessing a social structure which shared basic characteristics with the colonies and nations of the Caribbean basin. In this way the U.S. South is dealt with as part of what Charles Wagley has called Plantation America[3] and it is argued that its problems of poverty and underdevelopment came from the same sources as did underdevelopment in such places as Guyana, Barbados, and the northeast of Brazil.

Essentially, then, this work represents an interpretive essay, suggesting a way of thinking about both black economic history and southern economic development. As such this study makes no pretense at being definitive or exhaustive. Rather, it is intended to be broad-brushed with the framework and hypotheses offered here subject to further refinement and research. Furthermore, important and interesting aspects of the working of the plantation economy are omitted from this study altogether. For example, in this book which addresses the origins of black poverty, little is said about the role played by whites in that economy. That omission, however, reflects only the limits of my own knowledge and a concern to maintain the thematic unity of this study. White sharecroppers did play an important role in the post-bellum southern economy and were victimized in many of the ways that black sharecropprs were. But though their story is worth telling, this is not the place where that task is done.

This manuscript has been produced over the course of several years. During 1974 I benefited from a research leave of absence granted me by Temple University. During these years I also profited from comments made on the manuscript by George Beckford, Richard DuBoff, Stanley Engerman, Robert Gallman, Eugene D. Genovese, Louis Ferleger, Louis T. Harms, Joan D. Mandle, Isadore Reivich, Judith Stein, Harold Woodman and Gavin Wright. It may be that none of these individuals will be completely happy with the final manuscript, but I would like to thank each of them for the help which they offered me.

CONTENTS

TABLES AND FIGURES

FIGURES

FOREWORD

Professor Mandle finds the roots of black poverty in the Southern plantation economy and particularly during the post-Civil War period. He brings together a large body of cartographic, census, and other statistical data garnered from many sources, especially from the 1910 report of the U.S. census on plantations. So far as I am aware, these data have never been put together and analyzed so completely and meaningfully as Professor Mandle does here. We may now know more than we have known before what the tenant plantation in the South was like up to and beyond World War I and what its significance for the nation was and still is.

There were what were called plantations in the early Roman Mediterranean world, but "the golden belt of plantations" around the world, as Francis Delaisi in *Political Myths and Economic Realities* (1927) called it, developed as an outgrowth of the expansion of Europe after the sixteenth century. An evolving world community has since transformed oceans into inland seas and established dominant investment and trade centers in western Europe which progressively organized peripheral areas overseas into regional divisions of labor supplying raw materials to these centers for processing and marketing. In certain of these satellite regions, particularly those in tropical and semi-tropical climatic zones, agricultural staples such as sugar, tobacco, and cotton came to be produced for export through the instrumentality of an institution which, in the Portuguese and English tradition, was known as a plantation.

What kind of an institution is the plantation? It is an institution because it was structured around a centuries-long problem, the problem of labor. At least in America it manifested itself as a means of settling land and bringing it into new and presumably higher uses, in the production of agricultural staples for export, in

coerced labor rationalized on the principle of race, and in a
distinctive culture. It was something more than a feudal institution and something less than a capitalistic institution; Professor
Mandle prefers to speak of it as a "plantation economy," as a third
something, having its own dynamic pattern responding for profit
to an external market but resorting to nonmarket labor mechanisms. In the South these mechanisms have ranged historically
from white indentured servitude, to black slavery, to white and
black sharecropping.

When studied historically and around the world the plantation
appears in frontier situations where there is more land suitable for
staple crop production than there is labor to cultivate it. It functions in such situations as a means of bringing order out of more or
less disorderly conditions in behalf of economic motives oriented
toward external markets, and it continues as a symbol of order. In
its most obvious and visible aspects it appears as a number of
acres, growing crops, workers' quarters, and a manor house with
trees, but in its essential nature it far transcends these material
facts. The chief earmark of the institution is not to be found in its
economic purpose, as important as that is, but in the kind of
relations of interdependence between the people who live and
work on it. It presumes the existence of a collectivity in which
superordinate management and subordinate labor are necessary
parts. Of course, there is nothing unique about this fact—it is true
of Western industrial institutions generally—but there is something distinctive about the kind of statuses and roles assigned to
each part in the accomplishment of an economic purpose on the
plantation.

Everywhere in plantation society the idea of race comes to
enter, in some degree, into the definition of these roles and
statuses. The idea was carried to an extreme extent in the plantation society of the American South whose black slave population
was virtually read out of the human family. Everywhere the
plantation appears as a race-making situation, not only where
European whites and African blacks confront each other, but even
where planters and workers of these complexions are entirely
absent. But, whether for good or for ill, is it not true in every

political institution of whatever kind, from the state on down, that authority rests upon some commonly accepted mythological or ideological justification? In the case of the plantation almost everywhere race seems to supply that presumed justification. The unsavory reputation of the plantation in the modern world derives from the fact that race and caste are no longer accepted as bases of worker subordination and exploitation. We no longer are disposed to recognize any explicit racial "right" to command nor any explicit racial "obligation" to obey. The decline of the plantation in the South and around the world has followed the rejection of such alleged rights and obligations and their replacement by milder forms of social deference.

I think we miss what probably was most important about Southern plantation society, whether in the Old or New South, if we think of it only as a *system of plantations*, that is, as an array of plantation by plantation by plantation. Rather it was a *plantation system*, and there is a world of difference between the two expressions. It was a system in which the core institution, the plantation, was sustained and supported by a whole series of satellite institutions: the family, the coastal city factor, the church, the school and college, and state and local governmental units. It was a system geared to support and maintain not only the plantation economy narrowly conceived, but a whole order of society at the center of which the ideology of race lived as a deeply believed in principle of certainty equated with belief in God himself, especially by the master race.

The plantation system survived the Civil War and has to be the context within which Professor Mandle carries on his account of the natural history of the plantation in the post-bellum South. Implicit in this system was the white Southern world-view of which he speaks, that vision and outlook upon the universe characteristic of a people of which, in this case, race and paternalism were central aspects.

Professor Mandle focuses upon the labor mechanisms of sharecropping and tenancy which came to replace slavery after the Civil War. Sharecropping was established as a sort of compromise between, on the one hand, the desire of the freedmen to escape

the slave gang labor mode of work and, with his family, to live on
and cultivate a "farm" or tract of land apart from other tenant
families, and, on the other hand, the purpose of the planter to
make all decisions incident to planting, cultivating, and marketing
the crop. But the compromise did not prevent the individual
sharecropper from being an almost interchangeable part of the
machinery of plantation organization. In spite of certain legal
distinctions, one tenant was very much like another so that the
very high rate of tenant turnover each year made little practical
difference so far as the planter was concerned and even worked to
his advantage. For the sharecroppers themselves, on the other
hand, the precipitate of tenancy in the plantation South was
homelessness, and homelessness meant rootlessness. After years
of moving from one plantation to another in search of opportunity
and liberation it finally was not too difficult to make the great
move to the cities of the North. Professor Mandle documents this
massive migration which continued for several decades mainly
during and following World War I. This migration meant that,
unlike developments in certain European countries with semi-
feudal backgrounds, such as Denmark, Ireland, and France,
estate tenancy in the plantation South did not evolve into a
condition of peasant proprietorship to any considerable extent.

Professor Mandle's account of plantation tenancy in the post-
Civil War South parallels the presentation of quantitative data
with insightful observations of economic and cultural changes
which inevitably occurred. The culture of a people tends to take
any particular moment in time as final, but, of course, this is never
true; one stage sets the stage for the next one which will come no
matter what. The existing culture pleads for itself and tries to
stave off changes that threaten a way of life or to modify them
when they do come. In the tenant Plantation South the legal
control of labor-as-slaves gave way to planter control over land and
the food supply as the customary means of controlling and
stabilizing the labor of sharecroppers. The old habits of paternalism were diminished in strength but were not destroyed. The
obsessive preoccupation with cotton and tobacco, particularly
cotton, had long before transformed these botanical annuals into

institutional perennials subject to a carefully planned continuity from year to year. It was a tradition which had always used hoes and plows along with a partnership of mules and blacks. As U.B. Phillips noted, there had been a period of technological advance in plantation agriculture in the early years of the nineteenth century, but the steady addition of cotton acreage as planters moved west halted this and by the time of the Civil War cotton planters were locked into a customary mode of cultivation which effectively resisted technological advance as a threat to labor recruitment and control.

After emancipation, however, legal freedom had to be reckoned with, and freedom meant then what it always is, freedom to move. And in time freedoms to move reduced dependency to deference and deference to escape from the land of Egypt to the promised land of the North. The plantation economy cracked under the strain of World War I when "us angry Saxons," black and white, planters and tenants, were mobilized to fight the Germans. It cracked even more when thousands of black sharecroppers moved north after 1918 and still more during the depression of the 1930's and eventually World War II. Counter-plantation ghettoes developed in the cities of the North and even of the South which became centers of assault on the ideology of white surpremacy.

Now the old tenant plantation economy, facing acute labor shortages, was forced to turn to mechanization, to expensive cotton-picking machines and tractors fueled by gasoline instead of hay and corn. Mechanization has meant the return of the relatively large production land unit under proprietors who buy, rent, and combine smaller farms into units large enough to afford expensive machinery. There is still another consequence of mechanization: cotton production has moved into the Southwest, to the plains of western Texas, Arizona, and California. The Old South has merged into the modern Sunbelt.

"The black experience in the United States . . . has never been disassociated from the North," says Professor Mandle. The same assertion might be made of the Southern white experience, and Professor Mandle's book will make the Southern reader of either race more aware than he otherwise might be of the enduring role

of the North in the definition and role of the South from the
Revolutionary War to the present. For the most part it has been a
role of defense and dissent and negativism, a role which now in
the light of recent political and economic events may be changing
to a more positive one. But to a far greater extent than Portugal
was to Brazil or France and England were to their plantation
islands in the West Indies, the American North has been a chronic
Southern "problem." As Rome had its Carthage which finally it
was able to destroy, the South has never been able to destroy or
even to defeat its adversary, the North. On the contrary—the
South is incompletely described and understood if the North is
left out. He is a white Southerner to the extent he long has been
aware of "those people," as General Lee called them, somewhere
"up there" irritatingly critical of himself and of his way of life. They
invade, they send down their missionaries and carpetbaggers
uninvited, and they interfere with his relations with blacks. The
people of the North do not seem to have been equally preoc-
cupied, except occasionally, with the Southern presence.

Professor Mandle's book deserves the careful attention of any-
one interested in the background of black poverty in the United
States.

EDGAR T. THOMPSON
Duke University

July 1978

THE ROOTS OF
BLACK POVERTY

It [the plantation system] indeed was less dependent upon slavery than slavery was upon it; and the plantation regime has persisted on a considerable scale to the present day in spite of the destruction of slavery a half century since. The plantation system formed, so to speak, the industrial social frame of government in the black belt communities, while slavery was a code of written laws enacted for the furtherance of that system's purposes.—Ulrich B. Phillips, "The Decadence of the Plantation System," The Annals, *Vol. XXXV (January-March, 1910).*

I. THE PLANTATION MODE OF PRODUCTION

In this study the mode of production is used as a tool in examining the historical origins of contemporary black poverty. The disproportionate existence of poverty among blacks in America today will be taken as granted and will need no documentation. The problem is: What in the historical experience of the black population in the United States is responsible for the deprivation which currently exists? The answer to this question resides in the historical circumstances in which blacks found themselves. This means specifically their post-emancipation presence in the American South and the role they played in the southern economy. In that economy they constituted the lowest income population in the poorest region of the country. To know why southern blacks were positioned in this way is the task which we set for ourselves. To answer this question it is necessary to explore the structure of the southern economy and society. Hence there is a need for the construction of a model corresponding to the society in which the blacks found themselves.

The concept of the mode of production is central to Marxist social science. This phrase describes the model constructed by Marxists of the society under examination. As in all social sciences, the purpose of constructing such a model is to capture the dominant variables which are operative and on this basis analyze the most important sources of change in that society. What distinguishes the Marxist model from other efforts is the consensus which exists among Marxists with regard to the content of the mode of production.

In the Marxist tradition, two separable sets of variables have come to be considered the component elements of the mode of production. They are: (1) the forces of production, representing roughly the state of technology and the stock of plant and equipment as well as the labor force present in the economy; and (2) the relations of production, a concept which includes both the ownership structure of the society's productive equipment and the relationships that are established between the owners of capital and the workers. Thus, Maurice Dobb, citing Marx writes:

> . . . by mode of production he [Marx] did not refer merely to the state of technique . . . but to the way in which the means of production were owned and to the social relations between men which resulted from their connections with the process of production.[1]

In its classic formulation the relations of production and the forces of production are said to correspond to each other, with advances in technology inducing changes in the social organization of production. These organizational changes, in their turn, have a feedback effect on the technological capacity of the society. Thus a model showing the interaction of technology and the organization of production can be constructed. By examining the dynamics of the model, insight into changes in the real world which correspond to the model can be developed.

In recent years, two specific challenges to the formulation of the capitalist mode of production offered by Dobb have been issued by scholars who work within the Marxist tradition. Both essentially argue that Dobb's formulation, by omitting certain key variables, has allowed central sources of change to escape from the model. One of these challenges is associated with the work of Eugene D. Genovese; the other is associated with the works of Emanuel Wallerstein and André Gunder Frank. We deal with each in turn.

Genovese accepts the essentials of Dobb's formulation of the mode of production. His concern, however, is to correct what he calls "the tendency within Marxism . . . toward economic determinism which when unchecked does violence to the essentials of Marxian thought."[2] To do so he moves to at least an implicit critique of the Dobb formulation. The latter in specifying the component elements of the mode of production pays no attention to the role of culture and ideas. By omission, ideology and culture are assigned a derivative role, and as such, in a model in which only the most important causal variables need be identified, they are not discussed. In this Dobb follows the traditional Marxist view in which cultural questions are assigned to a superstructure which is dominated by the economic base of society.

Genovese, however, invokes the authority of Gramsci in offering as an alternative to the base/superstructure analogy the formulation of a "historical bloc." He points out that not only did Marx believe that ideas grew out of social existence, but that they, as well, took on a life of their own and had a feedback effect on the dynamic of the society. This causal role of culture is not made clear when it is assigned only a superstructural role. Genovese writes that a Marxist analysis:

must recognize the sociological uniqueness of every social class as the product of a configuration of economic interests, a semi-autonomous culture and a particular world outlook; and it must recognize the historical uniqueness of these classes as the product of the evolution of that culture and world outlook in relation to, *but not wholly subordinate to*, those economic interests.[3]

Though Genovese does not actually say so, it would seem to follow that in specifying the component variables of a mode of production an explicit formulation of the dominant world view and culture is necessary in order to be certain that all of the important causal elements are included.

To say this is by no means to solve some very difficult problems of cultural analysis. First, there is the need to delimit and define the relevant cultural sphere for inclusion in the model or mode of production. In this regard Genovese cites Gwynn Williams' paraphrasing of Gramsci's formulation of cultural or ideological hegemony as:

an order in which a certain way of life and thought is dominant, in which one concept of reality is diffused throughout society in all its institutional and private manifestations, informing with its spirit all taste, morality, customs, religious and political principles, and all social relations particularly in their intellectual and moral connotations.[4]

The dominant world view thus shapes what people believe to be common sense, right and good, and in this way, it is argued, hegemony plays a causal as well as a derivative role in the evolution of particular societies.

How strong and dominant—indeed, how autonomous and independent—this role of culture is becomes the crucial question in determining whether to include it in the mode of production. Unlike other spheres of social existence which are more readily susceptible to quantitative analysis, the precise extent to which ideological hegemony comes to prevail seems beyond precise measurement. Though its existence may be postulated, its relative strength may only be roughly approximated. As a result the causal weight which should be assigned to it must necessarily be left rather more unspecified than would seem to be desirable. Our inability to be precise with regard to its causal weight, however, should not stand as justification for its exclusion from the model altogether. Its inclusion may disrupt the elegance with which we construct the causal flows. This, however, will be a small price to pay if, by its incorporation in the model, we are better able to understand the dynamics of the society under investigation.

Genovese has argued that paternalism was the dominant world view in the ante-bellum South and that the dynamics of that society cannot be understood without an appreciation of the autonomous importance of that world view. Conversely, he argues, that "the destruction of slavery meant the end of paternalism as the reigning southern ideal of social relations . . .", though he adds that "it did not mean the total disappearance of paternalism as an ingredient in social relations."[5] Formulated in terms of our model this seems to suggest that the importance of the paternalistic world view as an independent variable declined in the South after the Civil War. Genovese's hypothesis is that, while paternalism represented a world view which helped to hold the slave society together, its power to do so declined in the post-bellum era. In this study, we test that hypothesis, both with respect to the existence of paternalism and the strength of that outlook in determining the direction of change in the society in the post-bellum era.

In the other major challenge to Dobb, Frank and Wallerstein point to the wider international context in which a society finds itself as an important, but neglected, element in the definition of capitalism. Wallerstein's consideration of the mode of production occurs in the course of his developing a model of a world capitalist system. He comments approvingly on Frank's work in which capitalism is seen as a world system divided into component regions. Each sphere by virtue of its participation in the world market is considered to be capitalist, though they may differ with each other with respect to internal social organization. In Frank's work there are two zones—the metropoles and satellites; in Wallerstein's there are three—the core, the periphery and the semi-periphery.

Wallerstein defends Frank from the charge that his analysis is not Marxist because it does not specify the relations of production. Wallerstein's rebuttal is that "the 'relations of production' that define a system are 'relations of production' of the whole system." In Wallerstein's view, "free labor is indeed a defining feature of capitalism, but not free labor throughout the productive enterprises." Thus Dobb's emphasis on the use of free labor as a key defining element in a capitalist model is rejected. Free labor in the world system is employed but only "for skilled work in core countries whereas coerced labor is used for less skilled work in peripheral areas." To Wallerstein, "the combination thereof is the essence of capitalism."[6]

In Wallerstein's framework, regions are assigned specific economic functions which redound to the benefit of the core areas. The purpose of the framework is to cast light on the uneven spread of economic development throughout the world. Yet at least in the first of the four volumes of his study which has appeared, Wallerstein has offered no systematic accounting for differential rates of economic achievement. The only suggestion of why core areas advance more rapidly than peripheral ones in this period deals with the core's ability to build upon already existing advantages.[7] Such an argument is incomplete and does not provide an analytic foundation which accounts for the movement of periphery countries to the core or the decline of core countries to the periphery. In short, in developing a universal model, the source of change within that model is given scant attention.

Yet Wallerstein himself recognizes the existence of important differences among the participants in the world economic system he describes. He writes that each of the zones "developed different class structures, used consequently different modes of labor control and profited unequally from the working of the system."[8] This seems to suggest recognition of the kind of differences between core and peripheral areas which Dobb would have emphasized and would have considered constituted different modes of production. Wallerstein views these differences as less important, following from the more important development of an international division of labor.

What is not addressed in Wallerstein's discussion are the long-run implications of these differences or the circumstances under which these contrasting social relations may change and approximate those of the metropolitan areas. It is entirely appropriate, for example, to point to the creation of New World slave societies as a consequence of the emergence of the European economies and to note that these new societies contributed to the wealth of Europe. That, however, is where the analysis is left. Unaccounted for is the consequent course of development of those new societies, a course which almost certainly was, in its turn, decisively influenced by the unique social organization contained within each of the periphery regions.

Wallerstein, like Frank, seems to argue that mere participation in the international economy inevitably retards the development of the periphery. Why this is so is never made fully clear. Whether trade acts to stimulate or retard growth would seem to depend upon the ability of the society in question to respond to changing opportunities. Three responses are possible to a widening of market opportunities. First, an international market may expand, but the country may be unable to take advantage of the situation and production remains as before. Second, the response to the growing market may take the form of expanding output, but within the constraints imposed by traditional technology and social structure. In this situation we might say that growth, but not development, had occurred. Third, there may be a dynamic response to increased international trade with the implication of revolutionary change both in technology and the social relations of production.

The crucial point is that the effect of an expanding world economy on a particular country or region is largely determined by what goes on inside the society. It is this determinant role of internal social structure which Wallerstein misses in his emphasis on the causal role of the world economy. The result is that the specific response of any individual periphery cannot be predicted on the basis of the variables which Wallerstein includes in his model. In turn, this suggests the incompleteness of the model and the misplaced emphasis in it on the international division of labor. Rather than the international division of labor being the independent causal agent, it seems much more likely that the role that a country or region plays in international trade is itself derivative, following from the consequence of its mode of production. This view suggests, contrary to Wallerstein's, that trading partners may each possess a different internal social organization. These internal differences will account for the varying responses to widening trade, thus precluding the necessity of including international relations in the mode of production.

In constructing our model we will specifically include culture as an independent variable in specifying the mode of production as Genovese suggests, but the argument is much weaker for doing so with respect to international trade. This means that, along with the state of technology and the social organization of production, specific attention is directed to the dominant world view, and an attempt is made to determine the extent to which it was critical to the dynamic of the post-bellum southern society. Less important, and not part of the model employed, will be the location of the market which existed for the southern staple. To be sure, prevailing market conditions and prices will be important data to examine in order to understand the response of the southern system. But the response to changes in such variables will be mediated through a specific social organization, the model of which need not specify whether the market is internal or external.

The argument advanced in this study is that the variables specified above—class structure, technology and culture—suggest that parts of the South even after the Civil War more closely resembled societies in the Caribbean than in the northern United

States. The different mode of production which prevailed in the Caribbean region is characterized as a plantation economy in order to distinguish it from more conventional Marxist usage that describes societies as either feudal or capitalist or some combination of the two. To fail to treat a plantation economy as a distinct mode of production is to miss the unique construction and impact of this market-oriented but archaic social organization. Treating a plantation economy as different from either a capitalist or a feudal economy is also to suggest that because of their differing organizational structures the dynamic of a plantation economy is different than that of these other forms of social organization.

A plantation economy is defined as one in which the state of technology allows profit-maximizing, large-scale farmers to produce a staple primarily for an external market. That same technology, however, requires the use of more workers than profitably low wage rates would attract. As a result some nonmarket mechanism is required in order for the planters to be sure of a sufficient supply of workers to carry out profitable production. In turn, those nonmarket mechanisms help to define the class relations of the society. The culture which emerges reinforces these class relations.

This model of society approximates the structure of the postbellum South. As such, that society differed in significant ways from either a capitalist or a feudal society. With regard to the latter, Dobb defined feudalism as a system in which status and economic authority are rooted in land tenure in which "the direct producer (who was himself the holder of some land) was under obligation based on law or customary right to devote a certain quota of his labour or his produce to the benefit of his feudal superior." Central to the feudal mode of production, according to this view, was the fact that even the serf had a claim to land. Dobb cites Bloch in this regard, for the latter asserts that "the land itself [is] valued because it enabled a lord to provide himself with men."[9] Plantation economies in which labor power was supplied by slaves or semi-slaves with no claim to land as a productive asset, however, are organized differently from the system sketched by Dobb in his discussion of feudalism.

Nor is a plantation economy the same as a capitalist economy. Dobb, following Marx, defines capitalism as a system of commodity production in which labor is supplied to the productive units through a market. The two historic prerequisites for the emergence of this system were the concentration of productive assets in the hands of a minority class in the population and the simultaneous development of a "propertyless class for whom the sale of their labour power was the only source of livelihood. . . ." The growth of a class of workers alienated from the control of the means of production stands in contrast to feudal conditions where serfs are not propertyless. But the fact that the propertyless workers under capitalism provide their labor ". . . not by virtue of legal compulsion, but on the basis of a wage contract" equally distinguishes such a system from a plantation economy.[10] In both the plantation and the capitalist economy, labor survives by working with productive assets owned by property owners. But in a capitalist setting such workers are free to enter into and out of employer/employee contractual relationships, giving rise to the functioning of a free labor market. Such opportunities, however, are severely constrained in a plantation economy where the choice of where and for whom to work is largely dictated to the workers under a system of force and sanction designed to implement the planters' will.

Thus, a model that replicates closely the salient features of plantation-dominated societies does not correspond either to a capitalist or a feudal mode of production. In the discussion which follows, the components of a plantation mode of production are treated and specifically applied to the post-bellum South.

William O. Jones argues that plantations are "different from other kinds of farms in the way in which the factors of production, primarily management and labor are combined."[11] Specifically, plantations are characterized by the use of a plentiful supply of low-productivity/low-wage labor which is mobilized under the close supervision of management to achieve substantial private returns. Though suggestive, this is unfortunately as far as Jones goes in characterizing the class and social relations on plantations. By contrast, Edgar T. Thompson has noted that the managerial control required on plantations was such that the plantation "became not only an economic institution, but an institution of government, a political institution" as well.[12]

Plantations were instruments of colonization. The settling of the tropical and semitropical New World was accomplished in considerable measure by the ceding or sale of large tracts of potentially cultivatable agricultural land to individual landholders. Given the prevailing level of technology for the commodities which could be produced in these settings, profitable large-scale production could be carried on only by using masses of laborers. How to mobilize such numbers of workers became the key to successful production, in a region which extended from Brazil and the Guianas through the Caribbean and the Caribbean coast and into the southern United States.

That such a number of disciplined workers neither were indigenously available in this region nor would be forthcoming voluntarily from elsewhere quickly became apparent.[13] As a result, nonmarket methods of allocation and control became essential in order to carry out profitable production in large volume. Force was required to supply the manpower the plantations required, and continued coercion was needed after the workers arrived on the plantations to ensure that the goals of the plantations were achieved. These goals, to be sure, were the cultivation and sale of agricultural commodities. But the circumstances in which these ends were essayed were such that the planters, or their agents, were compelled to assume extra-economic authority. A plantation economy then is one in which profit-maximizing agricultural landowners depend upon some mobilizing mechanism, not simply the operation of a free labor market, to satisfy the need of their farms for disciplined unskilled workers in large numbers.

The threat of labor's vacating the plantations and the threat to profits which such a move potentially represented account in part for the planters' extra-economic authority. For in the New World circumstances, the threat of labor's leaving the estates was a real one. George Beckford writes in this connection:

The problem for the estates from the very beginning was how to secure adequate labor supplies and for this purpose the system of slavery was introduced.

Because of its extensive land requirements the plantation normally can be established only in "open resource" situations in which all of the land is not already in permanent settlement. But herein lies the problem, for the population resident in a situation of open resources is in a position to secure an independent existence on the land and is not then normally available for the plantation work. . . .[14]

But there was an additional problem which the planters faced. Even if there were sufficient numbers of workers available to them, complications were created because such workers had not been forthcoming voluntarily. As a result their motivation to work was, to say the least, highly suspect. Labor might be present, but the planters still had to induce these individuals to work for them.

It is because of these circumstances that Thompson argues that plantations are best defined not in terms of territory or even in terms of agricultural production, but in terms of the authority of the planter; where the authority of the planter ended so too did the plantation as a viable institution. For while the first and most important task for the planter was to bind the laborers to the estate at least for the duration of the crop year, the use of authority, as Thompson writes, was also essential in order "to secure production." Each plantation, then, became at least as much an authoritarian political institution as simply a business enterprise. Power was vested in the planter and employed to achieve the latter's economic advance. Thompson writes that in such a setting when a worker "steals, fights, assembles unlawfully, plots, marries secretly, indulges in fornication, has illegitimate children, spends his time in gambling, cock-fighting or courting, the planter suffers some loss or threat of loss."[15] As a result, laws and regulations, governing these and many other aspects of plantation life, were established, resulting in the plantation's developing a high degree of autonomy and sovereignty.

Slavery, of course, was the classic mechanism by which plantation economies were rendered viable. However, in many parts of the New World, plantation economies survived emancipation. Thus in some parts of the West Indies emancipation meant practically nothing to the social organization because of the absence of unutilized land. With legal freedom the ex-slaves had no alternative employment opportunities available to them and thus *de facto* were compelled to continue to work on the estates as before. In other parts of the West Indies, where land was available and where the ex-slaves did vacate the plantations, indentured immigration became the mechanism by which the plantation dominated societies remained intact.[16] In Trinidad, Guyana and, to some extent, in Jamaica, a state-supported program of immigration resulted in an annual supply of new labor above and beyond the supply which came from the resident population. In this way the plantations were provided with a sufficiently large and cheap supply of labor, independent of the operation of a local labor market. These immigrants were legally required to work for a specified number of years on sugar plantations, and it was this process, combined with official discouragement of the creation of alternative industries, which allowed the plantation to continue to earn profits on the old labor-intensive and low labor-productivity basis for more than a century after emancipation.

In each of these cases the essential social relations of production of plantation agriculture were retained: monopolization of the productive assets by a small planter class; a continued close managerial and supervisory role by this class which extended to "noneconomic" aspects of plantation life; production of a staple for external markets; absence of a vital domestic labor market; use of low-productivity, low-wage labor; and a highly uneven distribution of income.

What is essential to the functioning of a plantation economy is the existence of a nonmarket mechanism by which labor is mobilized in larger numbers and at lower costs for low-productivity agricultural work than would be the case with an operative free labor market. The specific form that the nonmarket mechanism takes is not determinant with regard to the existence of a plantation economy. In the West Indies, slavery, indentured immigration, and/or the artificial maintenance of monocultural plantation production all served to guarantee the labor force requirements of the plantation system, and all did so in the absence of a viable labor market mechanism. The adaptability of the plantation system is thus greater than is sometimes assumed, for wherever and under whatever circumstances such a mobilization occurred, the plantation, with its attendant symbiotic relations between the "modern" plantation entrepreneur and the "traditional" unskilled labor force, proved viable.

The thesis advanced here is not that slave emancipation made no difference to the functioning of the plantation economy. Similarly it is not that plantation owners were indifferent to the mechanism of social control available to them. The extent to which planters throughout the New World resisted emancipation is testimony to their concerns. Slavery more than any other coercive system vested juridical property rights in man to the planters and thus represented the most efficient coercive mechanism available to them. The point is, however, that, though most desirable from the point of view of the planters, slavery was not the only mechanism by which plantation agriculture could retain the labor force control essential to its viability.

The argument suggested in this study is that in the United States South, as elsewhere in the New World, the plantation economy was able to survive slave emancipation. As was the case elsewhere, the means by which the plantation labor force in the post-bellum period was confined to the estates were more indirect than had been the case under slavery. It is to these indirect means of labor force control in the post-bellum South that attention is directed in the next two chapters.

II. OBSTACLES TO BLACK MIGRATION

Two factors appear to have converged in the period after the Civil War to permit the continued viability of the plantation economy in the United States. First was the system of tenantry which developed. Sharecropping, or share-tenantry, provided to the plantations the labor force stability for the duration of the crop year which the use of wages did not. In addition, it provided a sufficient degree of landlord supervision and control to allow for profitable use of the existing labor-intensive technology in cotton. Second, access to alternative employment opportunities outside of plantation work was effectively curtailed for black workers. This was the consequence both of the slow growth of alternative manufacturing employment opportunities within the South and of the failure to provide agricultural land to the ex-slaves in the aftermath of emancipation. The confinement which resulted was reinforced by the massive immigration of Europeans to the United States which occurred in this period. This influx of laborers in combination with discriminatory hiring practices against blacks in the North and the discouraging of recruiting in the South produced a formidable obstacle to southern blacks' finding work outside of the plantation economy.

With slave emancipation, the plantation structure of the southern United States agriculture was thrown into a severe crisis. With slavery abandoned, it remained an open question whether the plantation could remain a viable unit of production. Certainly one alternative would have put an end to plantation agriculture. That would have been a program of land redistribution in which the ex-slaves would have been provided with an allotment of land and encouraged to engage in commercial farming. The reasons that such a program of radical reconstruction was not undertaken have been detailed elsewhere.[1] The point is, however, that in failing to widen the ownership structure of southern agricultural land substantially and especially by race, the basic social relations of the plantation economy which existed before the Civil War were permitted to continue to exist.

Even in the absence of a massive program of land redistribution an alternative method of labor allocation and supervision to perpetuate the plantation economy may not have emerged. What the failure to distribute land more evenly to the southern population did mean, however, was that the ex-slaves were not provided with a competitive alternative to plantation work. This failure then gave the southern planter the opportunity to develop new methods of nonmarket labor force control.

What the planters needed above all was a resumption of work on the part of the ex-slaves in numbers and involving costs not markedly different from what prevailed before the Civil War. As Oscar Zeichner puts it with respect to the efforts to resume production, "the chief difficulty arose in connection with the labor supply which was insufficient to meet the needs of the planters."[2] This problem, of course, arose from the planters' inability to command labor to work. Now some new mechanism of labor mobilization and control was needed if the plantations were to reassert their dominance in the region's economy. It appears that three such mechanisms were essayed in the area: (1) labor contracted through the operation of a market, (2) immigration, and (3) sharecropping. Ultimately it was the last technique which proved successful in meeting the manpower needs of the estates, and which permitted the plantation economy in the South to perpetuate itself.

In the immediate aftermath of emancipation, wages were used in an effort to attract labor to plantation agriculture. In this the planters were aided by the activity of the Freedmen's Bureau which actively encouraged ex-slaves to enter into contractual work relationships with plantation owners.[3] Despite this effort, however, wage labor failed to provide the manpower base essential to plantation agriculture. In the first place, the ex-slaves in the first moments of their new freedom were understandably reluctant to return to work for their ex-masters. This reluctance was further reinforced by the belief that they were to be the beneficiaries of a program of land redistribution. Zeichner quotes a letter from General U. S. Grant in 1865 complaining that the belief among the ex-slaves that land would "be divided among them . . . is seriously interfering with the willingness of the freedmen to make contracts for the coming years. . . ."[4] On the other side, many planters could not bring themselves to enter into contracts with their ex-slaves, with all that such an agreement would imply in terms of juridical equality.[5] Moreover, the very economic disorganization of the period meant that many planters were literally unable to offer wage rates high enough to attract labor. Finally, it appears that even where wage rates did serve to induce labor to return to work on the plantations, the plantations' needs were not satisfied. The degree of labor mobility implied by the operation of a labor market meant that the kind of stable and reliable labor force essential to plantation agriculture simply was not available under this method of labor allocation.

At the same time that they were attempting to reattract an adequate labor supply by using wage incentives, southern planters also tried to augment the region's labor force through immigration.[6] States such as South Carolina, Louisiana, Alabama, Arkansas, Mississippi, Tennessee, Texas, Virginia, and West Virginia all passed laws to encourage immigration, sent immigration agents to other countries, or set up immigrant agencies. Initially the effort was to import Chinese to replace the blacks on the plantations, but efforts were also made to recruit migrants from Europe and from among new arrivals in the northern part of the United States.

Generally these efforts also failed to provide the manpower base necessary for successful plantation agriculture to be carried out. According to Shugg, some Chinese were brought from Cuba and the Philippines but they ". . . soon deserted the plantations to become independent fishermen and truck farmers for the New Orleans market."[7] Similarly, the effort to use "Coolie" labor proved illusory, among other reasons because of the wage differential which existed for these immigrant workers in railroad construction work as compared to plantation labor.[8] Unwilling to subdivide the plantations into commercial family farms, the South was in a weak position to bid for the services of immigrants. Yet it was precisely this unwillingness to break up the plantations that was the source of the region's continuing labor shortage.

Sharecropping was the mechanism by which the plantations ultimately were able to acquire and administer an adequate labor force. However, uncertainty surrounds the exact process by which this system of labor force control emerged. It is clear that even before the Civil War ended, southern planters were searching for some method to reduce the geographic mobility of the ex-slaves. In his detailed analysis of the post-Civil War experience in Georgia, Brooks documents the failure of the wage system in 1869, but disputes the contention of the Freedmen's Bureau that by 1868 the share system had replaced wages as the means of attracting the labor force. From his account it appears that sharecropping as the dominant form of labor organization was only gradually adopted in Georgia between 1867 and 1886, though he concedes that by the late 1860s there had been ". . . a wholesale abandonment of the wage system."[9] From this it seems reasonable to speculate that the intial thrust toward sharecropping occurred in the late 1860s, but that it took some years thereafter for it to become the dominant organizational basis for plantation agriculture in the South.

In contrast to more conventional systems of tenantry, a substantial degree of landlord control is retained in sharecropping and share tenant arrangements. In a simple renter relationship the tenant pays a fee in order to gain access to land as a factor of production. In carrying out production, the renter in turn provides most, if not all, of the resources complementary to land and makes his own decisions with regard to crop selection and production methods.[10] In sharecropping or share tenant relationships, this situation is reversed. Little or nothing is contributed by the tenant to the production process aside from labor, and in return, managerial functions are left in the hands of the landlord. The dependency relationship between landlord and tenant on plantations is further reinforced by the method and timing of payment to the estate laborers. Since the cropper is not compensated until his crops can be marketed and payment in kind as rental is made, share farmers were continually in debt to the landlord or local storekeeper throughout the crop year. It was only at the time of the harvest that the books were reconciled and the workers free to migrate. Unlike a weekly or monthly wage payment system, migration by a cropper before the end of the crop year meant foregoing the entire year's earnings, less the credit advanced. The delay in payment thus allowed planters to cultivate their estates in the knowledge that migration before the end of the crop year would be minimal.

To argue that sharecropping inhibited mobility during the crop year, however, does not speak to the question of why, at the end of the harvest, the plantation workers did not secure employment outside of cotton cultivating. One traditional explanation of the relative immobility of southern black labor has hinged on the question of debt peonage. Peonage exists when the planter forbids the cropper from leaving the plantation because of debt. According to Pete Daniel, "if at settlement time, the planter told his cropper that he remained in debt and could not move from the plantation then the system became peonage." Though Daniel nowhere attempts to quantify the extent of such peonage, he does write that "by 1901 southern society had reached the point where a debt-labor system characterized by violence and the corruption or acquiescence of local police officers was openly tolerated."[11] The impression which emerges from this description is that enforced immobility was widespread and economically significant.

At the same time, however, at the end of the crop year perhaps as many as one-third of the sharecroppers changed the plantations upon which they worked.[12] The magnitude of such interplantation mobility raises a serious question about the economic significance of the peonage system as an inhibiting factor on labor mobility. The weakness in the peonage system in curbing mobility is explained by George Groh:

If a cropper grew discouraged with his debt he could sometimes shuck it off by moving on to another location. The former landlord might track him down and try to extract the money, but the cropper's only real asset was his labor, and if he had consigned that to another landlord, the whole thing became a lot of bother.

If the sum owed was small by a proprietor's standard the affair was often dismissed with a passing complaint as to the black man's irresponsible ways.[13]

Debt peonage may thus have been ineffective in confining individual croppers to specific estates. The fact remains that, when the annual process of sorting out residences and work places was completed, the industrial structure of the black labor force looked much as it had before, with little, if any, movmement out of the southern plantation cultivation of cotton. Specifically, therefore, it is important to know what forces, market or otherwise, were responsible for the fact that the southern black laborers remained concentrated in plantation work, even though they did move from one estate to another.

Within the plantation South, occupational mobility was limited both by the difficulty southern blacks experienced in gaining access to productive land and by the slow pace of industrialization in the region. As shown in Table 3 of Chapter IV, land ownership by blacks in the parts of the South dominated by plantations was highly restricted even when compared to other sections of the region. No study has yet been carried out to determine whether this differential access to land was the consequence of discriminatory practices in the sale of land or the inability of blacks to raise the funds necessary to purchase valuable black belt property. In either case, however, the effect was to help confine black workers to the status of plantation workers, rather than to open up independent commercial farming as an occupational alternative.

Similarly, industrialization in the South provided little opportunity for blacks. Between 1890 and 1910 manufacturing employment in the United States as a whole increased by 5.6 million. Of these additional jobs, however, only 381,000 were located in the six states where plantation agriculture was most important— Alabama, Arkansas, Georgia, Louisiana, Mississippi, and South Carolina.[14] Even if no discrimination in hiring was practiced—an assumption of heroic proportions—it is clear that southern industrialization provided only a limited opportunity at best for blacks to escape the confines of plantation life.

In the North, of course, industrialization was proceeding apace. But there the demand for labor was satisfied by international migration rather than by blacks emigrating from the South. Between 1861 and 1900 14 million immigrants landed in the United States. Brinley Thomas has written that during these years "the ability of the Negro to establish himself in the North was conditioned by the volume of immigration."[15] In particular, opportunities for blacks in the North increased only when immigration slowed and opportunities decreased when the inflow of migrants picked up. In short, though immigrants and southern blacks were both potentially available for northern industrial employment, invariably it was the immigrants who were selected for these employment opportunities.

Once again, no systematic investigation has been made to sort out the reasons for this preference by northern capitalists, and in particular to identify the importance of racial discrimination in this experience. Robert Higgs, however, has provided evidence which casts light on this problem. He has carried out two statistical tests of discrimination in the setting of wage rates for European immigrants on the one hand and for native-born blacks on the other.[16] In both cases Higgs allowed literacy and the ability to speak English to be an index of skill. He found that variations in these two variables accurately predicted differences in observed wages for the immigrants, tending to suggest that discriminatory practices were relatively unimportant in determining immigrants' wage rates. On the other hand, a similar test of black wages in 1909 found that these same indicators of skills predicted wage rates substantially above the level which was actually paid. This result is consistent with the hypothesis of racial discrimination in the setting of wage rates for blacks.

In combination, these two results suggest differential employer attitudes toward European migrants and native-born blacks. As such this, in turn, is consistent with the view that it was racial prejudice which determined the employers' preferences for Europeans rather than blacks. The apparent fact that blacks were less equitably dealt with than immigrants in the determining of wage rates suggests greater hostility to one group than the other. It thus lends plausibility to the hypothesis that it was this difference in attitudes toward the two groups which accounted for employers' desiring to hire Europeans rather than blacks.

Even if northern employers desired to hire southern black laborers, a formidable disincentive to do so was constructed in the South in the form of legal recruitment barriers. These took two forms. First, several southern states such as North Carolina, Alabama, Georgia and South Carolina passed "false pretense" laws. The purpose of these laws was to keep agricultural laborers on the plantations for at least the duration of their contracts. Second, "anti-enticement" laws were designed and passed to minimize efforts by potential employers to seek out such workers. To prevent active recruiting of black laborers especially by industrial entrepreneurs from the North, states such as Alabama, Georgia, Mississippi, and South Carolina passed legislation to prohibit the "enticing" of croppers from their employers. According to Zeichner, in order to eliminate recruitment from the North the plantation states of Alabama, Georgia, Mississippi, and South Carolina "place prohibitory restrictions upon employment agents who solicit and send labor out of the states."[17] In addition, recruiters were subject to annual licensing fees at both the local and state levels and, in some cases, were required to post a bond to cover the debt owed by the laborers which they recruited. Zeichner summarizes his review of these laws by concluding that "the laws dealing with labor contracts, false pretenses, emigrant agents and the enticing of laborers have assured the planter of legal support in his effort to secure a stable labor supply during the agricultural year."[18]

Thus, four mechanisms have been identified that tended to confine black laborers to plantation work. Within the South, blacks had little access to land ownership, and industrial employment grew but slowly. Outside of the South, discriminatory hiring practices probably worked to the detriment of blacks, and northern employers were legally discouraged from recruiting black workers. Each of these tends to work in the same direction: to deny southern blacks access to alternative employment opportunities to plantation labor. With the exception of the failure of southern industrialization each represents "imperfections" in the labor market since each acts to limit black access to alternatives to employment in cotton.

The denial of access to southern agricultural land, discriminatory hiring practices in the North, and antirecruitment legislation made escape from plantation labor for blacks much more difficult than would have been the case in the absence of such market imperfections. The precise quantitative significance of these mechanisms either singly or collectively at this point appears impossible to measure. That they were significant, however, is a reasonable hypothesis in light of two facts. When given the opportunity to migrate to alternative employment opportunities during and after World War I, southern blacks moved with alacrity. Also, within the confines allowed them even in this period, black mobility was substantial. Thus, the hypothesis emerges that it was these barriers which constrained black occupational mobility out of the plantation economy rather than a voluntary choice.

The limit on economic choice which these three mechanisms represent suggests substantial constraints on the functioning of a competitive market for the black labor force in the plantation South. The result of these constraints was to create a larger supply of low-cost laborers to the plantations than would have been the case in their absence. In this way, their effect was to achieve precisely what other more directly coercive institutions of other plantation economies had accomplished. Industrial mobility was more difficult under slavery or under the system of indentured immigration employed at this time in parts of the Caribbean than under the less systematic pattern of the post-bellum South. Nonetheless, the mechanisms operative in the United States in large measure did deny to black labor access to alternative employment and thus confined them to plantation labor. In so doing the requirements of the plantation system were satisfied and the plantation economy was thus permitted to survive in the post-bellum era.

It is this wider context—mobility within the industry but coercion constraining blacks from shifting out of the plantation economy—which is missed in the recent proliferation of analytic work that has been done on the post-bellum southern economy. For example, Joseph D. Reid, Jr., in examining the economics of sharecropping argues that share arrangements were mutually more satisfactory to both the tenant and the landlord than the use of wage payments or money rentals. For the tenant, share arrangements meant an escape from the gang labor system associated with slavery. At the same time, the planter benefited from the increased supply of labor which was provided by sharecropping, while not being required to forego the close supervisory arrangements essential to plantation agriculture. In addition under sharecropping the planter benefited because the cropper was compelled to share some of the risks associated with production. From this, Reid concludes that competitive market mechanisms were operative within sharecropping arrangements and thus no misallocation of resources was likely to result from its adoption.[19]

In another instance Stephen J. DeCanio takes up the question of whether black labor was exploited in the post-bellum South. In this case, exploitation is defined as a situation in which the income received by labor is less than the marginal revenue product of labor. DeCanio, by observing that share contracts typically called for between one-quarter and one-half of the output to be received by the cropper and by calculating that the input elasticity of labor was in the same range, concluded that exploitation was not present.[20]

In both instances, these writers fail to deal with the wider context in which the market responsive behavior they are studying occurred. If it is true, for example, that black laborers and planters were able to agree on sharecropping as a mutually agreeable institutional arrangement, it is important to specify the circumstances in which this agreement occurred. This is important because in the circumstances of the South and in particular in the absence of alternative employment opportunities, the bargaining strength of black labor was relatively weak. What was acceptable to southern blacks was a function of the alternatives available to them. Presumably, therefore, sharecropping was acceptable in the coercive circumstances of the South only because other more desirable options were not available to them, a fact which Reid in his discussion of the bargaining which led to the mutually agreeable terms of the share contract does not mention.

In DeCanio's case the question which arises is exactly what significance should be attached to the finding that the marginal product of labor and the share of output received by labor tended to equal each other. This finding is the logical consequence of noting that within the cotton economy, planters competed with one another for the services of labor. But it says nothing whatsoever about the level of the compensation received by the plantation workers. Even if DeCanio's findings are accurate, they shed little light on the question of black poverty. This is so because entirely missing from his analysis is any consideration of the determinants of why both labor productivity and the compensation at which such workers were willing to provide their services were as low as they were. To consider the problem of black poverty it is necessary to deal both with the determinants of labor productivity in cotton and the existence of noncotton employment opportunities. If productivity had been higher, and/or alternative occupations had been available in large numbers, compensation in cotton would have been higher than it was. DeCanio's analysis is confined, in short, to a consideration of whether there was a market tending to equilibrium, rather than to a consideration of the determinants of the level of that equilibrium. Whatever else may be said about his discussion, because it fails to consider either the question of plantation labor productivity or black employment alternatives, it sheds little light on the question of poverty, which was the plight of most black agricultural workers.

In Chapter V the problem of productivity in cotton is discussed. The analysis carried out to this point, however, does address the question of why black labor was available so cheaply to the plantations. The thesis presented here is that the combined effects of the relative unavailability of land, racism, immigration, obstacles placed in the way of recruitment, and limited industrialization in the South tended to limit the occupations for which black workers could successfully offer themselves. In some instances, constrained by debt, that search for employment was limited by the crop cycle and the black workers' commitment to remain on the plantations through the harvest. They were denied access to agricultural self-employment within the region; meanwhile the competition for employment outside of the South was overwhelming. As a consequence, many southern blacks in effect were compelled to work on southern plantations. The compulsion was not juridical as it had been under slavery, and within the plantation sphere they showed themselves to be mobile and market-responsive. Nonetheless, the foreclosing of alternative occupational opportunities meant precisely that this market participation was effectively confined to the plantation sphere. Black labor in large measure was compelled to work in the cotton industry. At once, black labor's bargaining strength and therefore income were severely limited while at the same time the plantation mode of production was rendered viable.

III. THE CULTURE OF PATERNALISM

Sharecropping and share-tenantry were not the same as slavery. However effective the denial of alternative employment opportunities was in binding blacks to the estates, this mechanism did not provide the planters with the same degree of authority which slavery had. Thus, although there was continuity, there was also change, and in some important ways the post-bellum plantation economy was a good deal weaker than the slave system of the old South.

One key to the problem of comparing the prewar and postwar plantation economies centers on the mechanisms by which planter dominance manifested itself. Officially sanctioned force was a central element in the master-slave relationship in the old South. Yet, although force represented the ultimate sanction available to the slaveowners, its utility in maintaining a smoothly functioning society on a day-to-day basis is open to question. It is in this connection that Genovese has emphasized a world view partially shared by both slaves and planters, rather than force alone, as the mechanism which allowed the society to exist without continual violence. This hegemonic world view involved a system of paternalism in which masters dominated slaves. But it also implied a set of reciprocal obligations that, on one hand, acknowledged the humanity of the slaves but that also legitimated the dominance of the planters. To be sure, the use of force lurked just below the surface, and its use was all too real. But the resort to violence was not without its costs to the planters since its use risked a potential reaction by the slaves; nor was it entirely free of legal responsibility. Even in the slave society the use of force was not uninhibited and therefore not the exclusive basis upon which planter domination was achieved.[1]

Similarly in the post-emancipation period paternalism was an important source of planter strength and a foundation upon which the plantation economy rested. Thus Myrdal as late as the 1940s was still able to write:

. . . the South is a stubbornly lagging American frontier society with a strong paternalistic tinge inherited from the old plantation and slavery system. Paternalism is cherished particularly as the ideal relation between whites and Negroes. The Southerner is proud of his benevolence toward Negro dependents but would resent vigorously their demanding this aid as a right.

He goes on to argue that this paternalism ". . . is based on a clear and unchallenged recognition from both sides of an insurmountable social inequality," acceptance of which allowed for short-terms gains by the southern blacks while at the same time the social standing and superiority of the patron were reinforced.[2]

Several commentators have noted that the acceptance of this deferential world view was the necessary condition for southern blacks to achieve the status of landowner. Arthur P. Raper in his discussion of two black-belt counties in the 1930s argued that the single most important attribute of a successful black landowner was his acceptability to the dominant community. Raper goes on:

Being acceptable here is no empty phrase. It means that he and his family are industrious and that his credit is good. It means that he is considered safe by local white people—he knows "his place" and stays in it. Though it varies somewhat from one community to another and from one individual to another, the definition of "his place" hedges the Negro landowner about by restrictions similar to those which define and enforce the chronic dependency of the landless Negroes. . . .[3]

Indeed the sale of land itself was an act of patronage. Couch argues that "often the purchase will have been made at the suggestion of a white man who wishes to do a favor to a Negro whom he likes." By rewarding socially acceptable behavior in this way, white landowners thus were able to influence the nature of community leadership which developed among southern blacks. As Couch goes on to say black landowners become "pillars in the local church, they are the school trustees, the lodge and society officials."[4] In short, those who emerged as black opinion leaders tended to be those who had accepted a subservient view of themselves in the wider society. They thus constituted a supportive prop to the plantation-dominated society, even as they opened up a space for their creative energies in that society.

Yet the paternalism which survived the Civil War was not the same nor as strong as the paternalism which existed under slavery. For the reality to which the ideology of paternalism corresponded, the ownership of slaves by masters had been destroyed. Genovese cites a Louisiana planter as giving expression to this change. In a deposition filed with the Union army the planter said, "When I owned niggers, I used to pay medical bills. I do not think I shall trouble myself."[5]

The need to enter into contractual relationships with southern blacks—albeit contracts unequally enforced and one-sided in their power relationships—was offensive to many planters and triggered a withdrawing of the benefits previously extended to slaves. A young Alabama planter in 1875 wrote that, "A decently bred white man was never designed to trade with a nigger" and went on to declare that "their assumptions of familiarity are absolutely insulting."[6] The assertion of rights by blacks was, as suggested above by Myrdal, met by a withdrawing of benefits. Roark shows that in the new labor contracts which were negotiated with tenants and croppers, planters specifically attempted to avoid certain paternalistic responsibilities which they had assumed under slavery. For example, they now excluded explicitly their responsibility for the costs of medical care, burial expenses, the cost of a Sunday preacher and rations for those who did not work. Roark concedes that "despite the magnitude of the pressures acting against paternalism, emancipation did not mark the end of feelings of genuine concern for one's laborers" and that "the aristocratic tradition did not die out with the old regime or even the old aristocrats." Despite this, however, he concludes that "there was a noticeable abandonment of paternalism" in this period.[7]

The evidence seems to suggest that paternalism did manifest itself in the post-bellum ideology. Within this context, however, the terms of reciprocal relations between blacks and whites may have experienced a sharp change in which economic calculation assumed increased importance. Submission was, of course, demanded, but now relations were on a more business-like basis. The failure to work hard was now punishable by eviction; conversely, appropriately deferential behavior might be rewarded with land ownership. In both instances, the parameters of paternalism had changed. Under slavery, sale, not eviction, was the means by which a planter discarded a disruptive worker, while the positive reinforcement of approved behavior could not have extended as far as a legal claim to land. Thus, although the negative sanction of the post-emancipation paternalism might have been even more severe than that under slavery, since eviction raised the threat of starvation but the sale of chattel did not, the positive side was more rewarding, providing at least the necessary condition for the emergence of black commercial farmers—land ownership.

The new paternalism of the post-Civil War period reflected the limited but nonetheless real changes which occurred in the plantation economy in the aftermath of emancipation. Dependency remained and was vital to the health of the plantation economy. At the same time, the nature of the relationship between planter and sharecropper or share-tenant was different from the relationship between planter and slave. Thus paternalism, though weakened, persisted, at once reflecting the changes which had occurred in class relations, but reinforcing the basic continuity of the plantation economy.

Lying behind the paternalism of the plantation economy was the use of force. Violence and intimidation, especially when directed against blacks, were not random and indiscriminate, but had the effect of encouraging deferential and discouraging egalitarian behavior by blacks. Thus Davis, Gardner, and Gardner in looking at the administration of whippings analyzed the pattern they found in the following terms:

Periodically there seems to develop a situation in which a number of Negroes begin to rebel against the caste restrictions. This is not an open revolt but a gradual pressure, probably more or less unconscious, in which, little by little, they move out of the strict pattern of approved behavior. The whites feel this pressure and begin to express resentment. They say the Negroes are getting "uppity," that they are getting out of their place and that something should be done about it. . . . A Negro does something which ordinarily might be passed over, or which usually provokes only mild resentment, but the whites respond with violence. The Negro becomes both a scapegoat and an object lesson for his group. . . . After such an outburst, the Negroes again abide strictly by the caste rules, the enmity of the whites is dispelled and the tension relaxes. The whites always say after such an outburst, "We haven't had any trouble since then."[8]

This quotation points to two conclusions. First, violence was employed in reaction to a violation of approved behavioral norms, particularly attempts to escape deferential patterns by southern blacks. Second, the use of violence was aimed at individuals who were the immediate object of wrath, but also had symbolic importance for other black people in the community. The ability to inflict violence on one individual symbolized the capability of inflicting such force on other people as well, and thus acted as a deterrent against attempts to introduce more egalitarian behavioral patterns.

Frequent use of violence, however, is suggestive of ideological weakness, not strength. For, where a world view assigning certain groups to subordinate and other groups to superordinate roles is strong, the use of physical coercion is not necessary. In these circumstances, individuals naturally behave in the way which both society and themselves expect and believe to be right; and thus the use of force is not normally necessary. To the extent that these implicit rules are violated, where deferential behavior is not automatic, comfortable, and logical, then there is evidence of a breakdown in the ubiquity of the dominant world view. The use of force becomes necessary to coerce the approved behavior, but signals the fact that there has been a weakening of the ideological consensus.*

Data on the use of violence and force in the plantation econ-

---

*In addition to the use of violence, discussed in the next paragraph, the decline in the strength of paternalism may also underlie the fact that it was only in the 1890s that restrictive legislation with respect to public accommodations was enacted throughout the South. Though too far beyond the scope of this study to warrant detailed investigation, the hypothesis emerges that the resort to legislative sanctions was a response to the fact that paternalism no longer was as successful as it had been in confining the southern black population to its assigned place in society. With this hypothesis the new restrictive legislation represented a response by the southern ruling class to the decline in the cultural hegemony of paternalism.[9]

omy are very poor and difficult to interpret. Even if provided with data on the number of acts of violence committed in a year, what proportion of all such acts a particular number represents or how wide the resulting circle of intimidation was as a result is hard to assess. The one act of violence for which fairly systematic data are available is for lynchings. In a study made by James Elbert Cutler (1905), he estimated that there were 1449 lynchings between 1882 and 1903 in the states of Alabama, Arkansas, Georgia, Louisiana, Mississippi, and South Carolina. Of these 83.7 percent were committed against blacks. During these years, then, there were on the average 69 lynchings per annum in these states, a figure large enough to suggest that blacks in these states knew that the threat of violence associated with nonconforming behavior was real.[10] But whether these data can be interpreted to suggest a weakening of paternalism remains dubious since we are uncertain with regard to their representativeness.

The reality of the ownership of humans and the responsibility associated with that ownership—if even only to secure production and profits—had both caused and reinforced a culture of mutual responsibilities. With slavery no longer extant, planter concerns with the welfare of southern blacks declined in association with the decline in ownership of this population. Similarly as the planter provision of amenities dropped off, the sense of obligation which blacks may at one time have felt, too, tended to dissipate. Thus, though paternalism was still present by the end of the nineteenth century, it was markedly weaker than it had been under the slave regime.

In addition to the ending of slavery itself, the emergence of a new type of business and community leader in the South seems to have also triggered a decline of the old culture. Having their roots in both the North and the South, these businessmen did not share the cultural values carried over from the slave period. They did not perceive a responsibility to southern blacks other than what was recognized through labor market relations. Paternalism was weakening in this period not only because agriculturalists responded in this way to the demise of slavery, but as well because new sectors of economic activity emerged, undertaken by

entrepreneurs whose value system largely lay outside of the
ideological world view which corresponded to the ante-bellum
system of slavery.

In this connection William H. Nichols writes that it was in the
post-bellum South that a new middle class of businessmen
emerged. He testifies that "as little islands of industrialization
began to develop in the towns after the Civil War, trade and manufacturing came almost entirely into the hands of new businessmen." Nichols argues that this new middle class increasingly
accepted community responsibilities and gradually displaced the
planter class in this regard. But the influence of this new group
was to "bring about economic and social changes for which the
whole depressed southern region had a crying need, whereas the
planter class merely sought to preserve a socioeconomically
intolerable status quo." In short, Nichols argues that this new
class "accepted a new principle of bourgeois oblige which was
more attractive—and certainly less paternalistic—than its mori-
bund aristocratic equivalent."[11]

At the same time northern influences came increasingly to be
felt in the southern economy. Once again, to the extent that new
sectors of economic activity were initiated by entrepreneurs
steeped in a value system formed outside of the traditional southern culture, paternalism was in relative decline. No quantitative
estimates exist of the penetration of northern capital in this region
in this period, but qualitative descriptions at least suggest that
such investment was of increasing importance. C. Van Woodward,
for example, has vividly described the penetration of the
southern economy by investors from the North, a process which
he dates from the late 1870s, and specifically from the 1877
Compromise. Areas of special attention for northern investors
seem to have been land sales and real estate, railroads, minerals,
timber, iron and cotton textiles.[12] With northern capital came
northern ways of life, thus undermining the traditional southern
paternalistic culture.

Paternalism, however, continued to exist, but in relative decline. As an essentially conservative world view it stands along-
side the role of discrimination in the North, the inability of south-

ern blacks to become substantial landowners, and anti-enticement laws in supporting the plantation economy. However, it is one thing to assert its existence but quite a more difficult job to estimate its relative importance among these other supports of the plantation economy as a mode of production.

It appears that at least as between the denial of employment opportunities in the North and the role of paternalism in confining blacks to plantation labor, the latter was by far the weaker influence. The impact of paternalism alone in the post-bellum period probably was insufficient, in the absence of other structural supports, to maintain an adequate supply of workers on the estates. Evidence to this effect is suggested in the circumstances under which the great migration northward of blacks was ultimately initiated at the time of World War I. In this case it is as if an experiment had been carried out in about 1914 in which the ideological variable can be assumed to have remained constant, but one of the structural variables had changed. Under these conditions we are able to observe the response of the population and infer whether the change in the one variable was sufficiently important to overcome the continuing influence of the other.

In this case the structural variable which changed was the presence of competing international immigration in the labor markets of the North. We will discuss the impact of the curtailing of immigration during World War I more fully in Chapter VI. Suffice it to say here, however, that with the shutting off of international migration, the demand for black labor in the North increased dramatically and southern blacks responded to this demand in great numbers. Such a response is suggestive of an interpretation which argues that the independent strength of the culture of paternalism, at least as it tied blacks to the plantations, was relatively weak. This, of course, tends to confirm Genovese's hypothesis concerning the relative weakness of post-bellum paternalism. The failure to move to the North in the period before the war must largely be assigned to structural rather than ideological constraints. For once the structural obstacle was removed, even though paternalism must have persisted, a great wave of migration ensued. It appears that however strong the conservative impact of paternalism may once have been, it was not by 1914 important enough to dissuade many southern blacks from seizing the opportunity for economic advance which the chance to move to the North symbolized.

It is in this context of plantation-associated poverty, paternalism, and coercion that we can assess Richard Wright's remark that, "perhaps never in history has a more unprepared folk wanted to go to the city."[13] What Wright was pointing to was precisely the problem for southern blacks in shifting to an industrial capitalist economy caused by an ideology, life-style and set of skills formed in the context of the plantation South. Prosperity in an industrial capitalist setting involves either filling an entrepreneurial role and benefiting from the prosperity associated with profits, securing a professional occupation which yields high incomes, or working as a skilled laborer and thus benefiting from high levels of labor productivity. Failing successfully to take one of these three routes means at best hard work and low income. But in each case the probabilities of southern blacks successfully filling such roles not only were limited by the racial discrimination they encountered in the North, but, in addition, by the legacy of having been raised and trained in a region dominated by plantation agriculture.

Obviously a professional career was foreclosed for most blacks because of the poor education and training they had received in the South.[14] For those skillful or lucky enough to secure such education, northern racial discrimination operated further to reduce professional opportunities. Similarly entrepreneurial functions were limited both because of a lack of experience in such roles in the South and northern whites' refusal to patronize black businesses. What remained as a possibility was work as a skilled laborer upon entry into the industrial economy. But the initial movement to industry in the United States occurred during World War I when international migration was curtailed. Southern blacks represented an alternative labor supply for those occupations formerly filled by European migrants. The problem was that these first generation occupations typically were low-skill, low-wage jobs. Thus, at least in the first instance, blacks as substitutes for Europeans were in demand for occupations which provided only low incomes.[15]

There are, however, interpretations which can be assigned to Wright's statement about black preparedness which should be resisted. Particularly it should be emphasized that black participants in the southern plantation economy were not "premodern" if by the latter phrase we mean unresponsive to market signals or unused to management-imposed discipline. Though plantations acted as an obstacle to technological advance, they nonetheless were profit-oriented, market responsive institutions in which labor was required to function according to the needs and dictates of the planters. In these ways the plantation experience was markedly similar to the factory experience though, to be sure, the pattern and rhythm of the work demanded by management was very different from factory work.

Similarly, market responsiveness was not new or unusual for participants in the plantation economy. This was especially true as we have seen in the post-emancipation economy where, at the end of the crop year, much intraregional migration occurred by the labor force in a search for enhanced economic standing. As we shall see, too, the speed with which southern blacks responded to the market opportunities which emerged in the North with the curtailment of migration to the United States suggests a population able to gain and evaluate economic information—a population both modern and market responsive.

The experience outside of the South was decisively influenced by racism; so, too, was it shaped by the fact that the movement north was to a capitalist society in which economic inequalities were built into the structure of the economy. But it is beyond the scope of this study to investigate the sources of racism in the United States. Similarly we do not try to account for the evolution and viability in the North of a capitalist economy characterized by chronic instability and gross differentials in income and wealth. It is sufficient simply to point out that the northern society into which southern blacks moved was racist, with all that suggests with regard to caste privileges, and capitalist with all that suggests with regard to class privileges. It was unfortunately true that the

immigrants from the plantation economy suffered both disadvan-
tages, the deprivations associated with race and the deprivations
associated with only being workers, not capitalists.

On this basis, we can make the following generalizations about
the black experience to about 1910. The plantation economy
dictated deferential behavior by blacks after the Civil War. Paternalism persisted and was functional to the economy in the South,
but it was less important than under slavery. The potential reward
for approved behavior now extended as high as land ownership,
while violence against "deviant" blacks persisted as a mechanism
of social control. As a result, black laborers in the South learned
the attitudes of modern workers—responsiveness to both management and the market. Thus the paternalism of the post-emancipation period seems to be of little importance in explaining
black poverty. Deference continued because it was demanded
and backed by violence; but poverty continued because blacks
were excluded from alternative employment opportunities by a
combination of market and nonmarket mechanisms. Deference,
in short, was the consequence of the circumstances which produced poverty rather than a principal factor in causing poverty.

IV. TENANT PLANTATIONS IN THE POST-BELLUM SOUTH

Unfortunately it is very difficult to locate quantitative data indicating the contours of the southern plantation economy in the years after the Civil War. In large part this absence of data results from the fact that the Census Bureau in collecting agricultural data normally treated each tenant farm as a separate entity. Only in 1910 did the Bureau alter its data-collecting methods and acknowledge that southern tenant farms were part of larger production units. In that year the Bureau issued a special study of plantations based on a survey of 325 rural counties in eleven southern states.[1] It is this source which provides our first comprehensive data on the relative importance of plantation agriculture in the region.

The 1910 study of plantations carried out by the Census Bureau included counties in eleven southern states. Not only does the study fail to enumerate the specific counties included in the sample, but it also does not specify the decision rules which were invoked in determining which counties to examine. It does, however, indicate that

... in the great majority of the counties for which plantation statistics are presented the Negroes constituted at least half of the total population, and that, on the other hand, there are comparatively few counties outside of the area for which plantation statistics are presented in which the proportion is as high as 50 percent.

At the same time the study affirms it included all counties in the South "... in which the plantation system is extensively developed."[2] The Bureau was quite explicit in acknowledging share and tenant farming as the new organizational basis of plantation farming. Its definition of a tenant plantation was:

. . . a continuous tract of land of considerable area under the general supervision
or control of a single individual or firm, all or a part of such tract being divided
into at least five smaller tracts, which are leased to tenants.[3]

On this basis, the Census Bureau identified 39,073 plantations
in 1910 in the counties under investigation. Of these plantations,
28,290 were in the six states of Mississippi, Alabama, Arkansas,
Georgia, South Carolina, and Louisiana. There are no data presented on the relative importance of plantation agriculture compared to other forms of farming by state, but the study indicates
that 33.4 percent of the improved agricultural acreage in the
counties of the eleven states which were studied were in plantations. In the six states mentioned above, plantation acreage as a
percentage of improved land came to 47.9 percent in Mississippi,
39.4 percent in Arkansas, 39.3 percent in Louisiana, 38.1 percent
in Alabama, 37.1 percent in Georgia, and 30.8 percent in South
Carolina. Mississippi and Alabama ranked highest with respect
to the absolute number of acres in plantation agriculture. The
former had about 3.2 million acres in estate cultivation and
Alabama had about 3.0 million acres. These two states alone
accounted for almost 40 percent (actually 39.3 percent) of the
total plantation acres reported in the study. Plantation acreage in
Georgia, Arkansas, Mississippi, Alabama, South Carolina and
Louisiana accounted for 82.1 percent of all plantation acreage.

With tenant farming the organizational basis for plantation
agriculture, southern estates typically were divided into two
components: a section which was farmed directly by the owner or
manager of the plantation and the remainder which was cultivated by the tenants or sharecroppers. The 1910 study found that
there were 398,905 tenant farms on the 39,073 plantations it investigated, an average of a little more than ten tenant farms per
plantation. It goes without saying that what the Census Bureau
called "landlord farms" were much larger than the tenant farms.
Average acreage for the former was 330.0 acres in contrast to 38.5
acres for the latter. At the same time, however, improved landlord acreage came only to 86.6 acres compared to 31.2 for the tenants, reflecting the fact that the tenants employed farm land
much more intensively than did the owners. By multiplying

average acreage per tenant by the number of tenants per plantation, and then dividing that number by the total acreage per plantation under cultivation, we learn that tenants were responsible for about three-fourths of the plantation acreage that was cultivated.[4]

Though the individual counties under consideration in the Census study were not identified, a map of the area containing all 325 counties was provided. By comparing this map with county maps of the states involved, we were able to identify the counties included in the study. Of the plantation counties, 270 were in the seven states of Alabama, Arkansas, Georgia, Louisiana, Mississippi, North Carolina and South Carolina.[5] We then were able to identify the remaining 298 counties in these same states as nonplantation counties and on this basis proceed to compare the experiences of these two groups of counties.

The plantation counties represented a region including some of the most productive land in the South. Included were the South Atlantic Coastal Plain, the Alabama-Mississippi Black Belt, the Tennessee River Valley in Alabama, and the lower Mississippi and tributary river valleys. Soil type varied considerably

TABLE IV.1. Improved Land in Plantation Farms by State for 325 Counties: 1910

Location	Acres
The South	15,836,363
Alabama (47 counties)	3,028,979
Arkansas (23 counties)	1,054,049
Florida (1 county)	47,577
Georgia (70 counties)	2,855,402
Louisiana (29 counties)	1,190,599
Mississippi (45 counties)	3,196,834
North Carolina (21 counties)	530,830
South Carolina (35 counties)	1,652,865
Tennessee (11 counties)	449,506
Texas (41 counties)	1,752,524
Virginia (2 counties)	77,198

SOURCE: U.S. Bureau of the Census, *Plantation Farming in the United States*, Table 14.

over these regions. C. O. Brannen, in discussing the soil conditions associated with plantation agriculture, however, indicated
that "plantation lands are practically always naturally fertile or
capable of being made highly productive by the use of commercial fertilizers and manures or by crop rotation."[6]

The 270 plantation counties under consideration here contained a population of 7,195,600 in 1910. Substantially in excess of 50
percent of this population, 3,933,627, was black, with this number constituting 40 percent of the black population of the United
States in that census year. By way of contrast the 298 nonplantation counties contained a population of 6,288,076 in 1910, slightly less than 30 percent of which was black.

That the role played by the black population in the two groups
of counties differed is suggested in Table IV.3, where information is provided on the distribution of black farms by tenure.
There it is indicated that while only about 13 percent of the black
farms in the plantation sample were owner cultivated, almost 40
percent of black farms in the nonplantation sample were black-
owned. This represents evidence tending to indicate that black
farmers found it much more difficult to achieve an independent

TABLE IV.2.   Percentage of Improved Lands in
Plantation Farms by State for 325 Counties: 1910

Location	Percentage
The South	33.4
Alabama	38.2
Arkansas	39.4
Florida	26.2
Georgia	37.1
Louisiana	39.3
Mississippi	47.9
North Carolina	19.6
South Carolina	30.8
Tennessee	23.7
Texas	20.0
Virginia	14.9

SOURCE: Table IV.1.

TABLE IV.3. Percentage Distribution of Black Farms by Tenure Status by Grouping of Counties: 1900

Tenure Status	Plantation	Nonplantation
Owner, part owners, owners and tenants, managers	13.3	39.2
Cash Tenants	48.4	25.1
Share Tenants	38.3	35.7

SOURCE: Bureau of the Census, *Census of the United States, 1900*, Vol. 5.

status in those areas of the South dominated by plantations than elsewhere in the region.

The plantation counties differed compared to the nonplantation counties also with regard to the extent to which their agricultural sector specialized in the production of cotton. As indicated in Table IV.4 between 1880 and 1910 cotton represented at least half the value of the agricultural output in the plantation counties, representing in excess of 70 percent in both 1880 and 1890. By contrast at no time did cotton in the nonplantation counties account for as much as half the value of agricultural production, reaching a low of only 24 percent in 1900.

In general, then, one group of counties differed from the other not only with regard to the presence or absence of the plantation form of agricultural production, but also with regard to the con-

TABLE IV.4. Cotton as Percentage of Value of Agricultural Production by Grouping of Counties: 1880–1910

| Year | Counties | |
	Plantation	Nonplantation
1880	71.3	42.6
1890	80.2	46.3
1900	51.6	24.1
1910	55.7	34.5

SOURCE: Bureau of the Census, *Census of the United States, 1880*, Vol. 3; *Census of the United States, 1890*, Vol. 5; *Census of the United States, 1900*, Vol. 5; *Census of the United States, 1910*, Vol. 5.

centration of blacks in the population, the role played by blacks in agriculture, and the extent to which the agricultural sector specialized in cotton cultivation. Thus, where plantation agriculture was concentrated, blacks found it most difficult to gain access to the ownership of land, which was typically employed in the production of the South's traditional staple.

The problem of labor force supervision and control in the absence of slavery was, of course, the key to the resumption of successful plantation agriculture in the post-bellum South. According to the conventional typology three different methods for mobilizing labor presented themselves. Planters could select either a wage labor, a rent tenantry, or a sharecrop system. Each, it usually is suggested, implied different levels of risk for the parties to the arrangement and involved contrasting levels of landlord supervision. Yet in plantation circumstances these easy distinctions, perhaps applicable to agriculture elsewhere, are not very useful. Differences in planter supervision and control in particular were not very substantial over these three types of labor/management relations. Planter prerogatives with regard to cultivation practices remained dominant in each. Especially as between sharecropping and other forms of tenantry the differences were minor and only a matter of degree, not kind. According to Brannen in the cotton plantation areas this degree of supervision "often amounts to the control of the cropper's or tenant's crop" and the direction of the workers' farming activities by the landlord or manager was similar in each of these tenantry systems. In general, Brannen notes that croppers or tenants "are referred to by the planters in much the same light as the laborers who receive a money wage."[7]

Generally, the use of wage labor was the least important means

TABLE IV.5. Percentage of Cultivated Plantation Acreage Worked by Wage Hands, Croppers, and Tenants, Selected Cotton Plantations: 1920

	Wage Hands	Croppers	Tenants
Cotton Plantations	18.7	30.9	50.4

SOURCE: U.S., Department of Agriculture, Department Bulletin No. 1269, C.O. Brannen, *Relation of Land Tenure to Plantation Organization*, October 1924, p. 21.

by which the plantations solved their labor power requirements. As noted in the previous chapter the principal difficulty in using a wage system was the unreliability of the labor force when such a system was employed. Thus Brannen as late as 1924 wrote that

. . . the supply of wage labor has been so uncertain and that which was available has been so unstable and unsatisfactory, that in many localities of the Cotton Belt little or no wage labor is employed other than the extra wage labor performed by the cropper and tenant families on the plantation.[8]

The bulk of the labor force on the plantation was provided by tenants and sharecroppers. But the word "tenants" should not be confused with simple renters of land. In the plantation economy, there were a variety of tenant agreements, many of which implied greater planter supervision than under a more traditional cash rental system. The most important of the tenant relationships was share-tenantry. In this, like sharecropping, rental was paid as a percentage of the crop produced. The difference between sharecropping and share-tenantry is that the cropper provided nothing but labor to the production process while the share-tenant did control farm equipment and work animals. That these two systems had much in common is suggested by a 1930s summary of field studies which indicated that "the difference between these two classes is simply one of degree."[9] Though the share-tenants generally were more wealthy than the croppers, Brannen noted that "supervision is not the basis for distinguishing the cropper from the tenant. While croppers as a class are closely supervised, yet the difference in this respect is of little consequence on the plantation."[10]

Sharecroppers and share-tenants represented the bulk of plantation tenants. In addition to these, standing-renters, renters who furnished practically everything to production except land in exchange for a fixed amount of the staple, were also present. According to a USDA survey in 1924, the standing-renter experienced close planter supervision in only 41 percent of the cases. This compares to close supervision in 81 percent of the sharecropping arrangements investigated and 61 percent of share-renter relationships.[11] Rarely, however, did the standing-renter relationship extend to as much as one-fifth of the plantation land

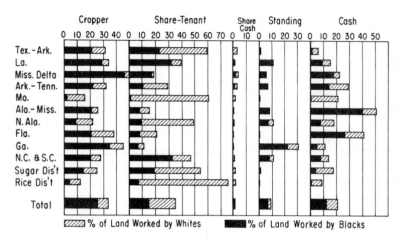

FIGURE IV.1 Percentage of Improved Land Worked by Cropper and Tenant Class in the Plantation Areas: 1919

NOTE: This diagram shows (1) proportion of improved land worked by the different classes of plantation labor in the various areas, (2) proportion of improved land in the 93 selected counties worked by the different classes, and (3) relative proportion of improved land in the areas worked by white and black croppers and tenants.

SOURCE: Brannen, *Relation of Land Tenure to Plantation Organization*, p. 35.

under cultivation. We may conclude therefore that in the overwhelming number of cases a system of planter/worker relations was established, usually sharecropping or share-renting, which allowed for wide-ranging planter supervision over the farms rented to the tenants.

A tenant system, in one form or another, was the means by which labor was supplied to the plantations. However, as this review suggests, by no means does this indicate that an independent peasantry had emerged in the South. The typical tenant arrangement—either sharecropping or share-tenantry—implied a high degree of planter supervision and control. These forms of tenantry at once therefore represented a system which provided a more reliable labor force to the planters than wage labor would have, but at the same time implied little diminution in planter authority. These tenantry forms were, in short, systems which satisfied the labor supply and control needs of a plantation economy.

The content of planter supervision was made clear in Morton Rubin's post-World War II anthropological study of the internal organization of plantations. He concluded that in addition to being a business enterprise, plantations were a "total sociocultural system." Within this system "the power structure of the plantation is authoritarian" in which a class/caste system results in a hierarchy running from a white owner at the top, through white and black supervisors and taskmasters to black tenants at the bottom. He goes on to argue that the power and authority of the planter "enable him to control the human factor in the situation to a degree far exceeding comparable institutions in a supposedly democratic society." This results ultimately in the fact that "the plantation remains a last vestige of beneficent despotism."[12]

Though the beneficence of this despotism can be denied, it is clear that great power was vested in the hands of plantation management and ultimately the plantation owner. Furthermore, the ubiquity of the planters' control of the lives of estate residents clearly exceeded that of industrial managerial prerogatives over a firm's labor force. The race/caste stratification system not only permitted those in authority to discipline black workers consistent with the economic functioning of the plantation, but it had cultural and political counterparts as well which also reinforced planter authority.

Aside from the use of violence, the ultimate sanction available to the planters was the denial of work and lodging to black workers and their families who overstepped the behavioral norms of the society. Tenantry had thus made plantation workers even more vulnerable to managerial authority than wage workers. A violation of behavioral norms in the intimacy of the plantation economy by a black worker would not only mean loss of work and residence, but would also make the securing of alternative arrangements in the proximate area difficult. Plantation residence also widened the range of behavior for which croppers and tenants were accountable to the planter. Schooling, religion and credit extension, as well as housing, were areas of worker activity which under capitalist industrial relations are not normally subject to direct managerial control, but which under plantation conditions were so controlled. Because estate workers lived on the plantations and these were essentially closed communities, these and other forms of "noneconomic" behavior affected the running and efficiency of the plantation and thus drew the careful attention of the plantation owner.

A normal work day on a closely supervised tenant plantation started with the ringing of a bell indicating that it was time to arise. Another bell, usually at sunrise, indicated the beginning of the work day and a bell at about sunset indicated the end of labor for that day. The land upon which the tenant worked had been assigned him by the landlord. Normally croppers cultivated land nearest to the headquarters of the plantation in order to facilitate landlord supervision. This supervision occurred during the daily rounds made by the farm manager in which he gave instruction on the details of field work. The tools with which the sharecropper worked were, of course, owned by the planters and were supplied out of a pool of such equipment.[13]

The key to the planters' power was the ability to supervise closely the production process. It is this managerial function that was responsible for the fact that sharecroppers and tenants were not really independent farmers. Donald Alexander cites a cropper as saying that "when you work on a white man's place, you have to do what he says or treat, trade or travel," to illustrate this point.[14] As a result, tenants did not have the opportunity to try out farming methods on their own and gain managerial skill and experience.

In addition to the supervisory system a second unique feature of plantation agriculture was the system by which credit was extended to tenants. Because of the lien attached to their crops share-tenants and croppers normally had no access to primary sources of credit. They, thus, were forced to secure advances from their own landlords. The latter extended credit typically in two forms: cash advanced and the provision of merchandise from a plantation store. Repayment of the loan occurred at the time the crop was sold. According to a 1926 survey of plantations in North Carolina 82 percent of croppers received cash advances from planters; the average interest charge on these advances was

21 percent. In addition, 60 percent of the croppers received household supplies through the extension of credit; the interest charge on these goods was 53 percent. Where plantation stores were not present, tenants gained access to household supplies from merchants on the landlord's guarantee; this was the most expensive form of credit with an average annual interest charge of 71 percent.[15]

Many tenants found themselves unable to repay their advances fully at the end of the crop year and thus found themselves in debt to the planter. In 1930, for example, 13.4 percent of cotton croppers finished the year in debt, averaging $110 debt per family. Interest charges obviously contributed to that debt. According to the 1928 North Carolina survey, interest payments came to more than 10 percent of tenant income. Woofter's investigators found that planters received cash loans from banks at 6.5 percent per year while extending loans to their croppers at 21 percent. The authors did not attempt to analyze the reasons for the high rates charged by the planters except specifically to reject the view that they were justified by the risks borne by the planters. In North Carolina losses to merchants and planters as a result of defaults on loans came to only 5 percent of the credit extended. Thus the difference between what the planters were charged by the bank, plus 5 percent and the rate charged to the tenant, was totally absorbed by the planters. Woofter simply concludes that "landlords and merchants are taking care to keep the interest rate well above any possibility of loss from defaulting tenants."[16]

It is hard to know whether these rates actually were usurious. But there were other aspects besides the interest rate charged which in the plantation credit system served the purposes of the planters in restricting the mobility of croppers and tenants. Credit can be a means to economic advance and growth. When available at relatively low rates and employed for the purchase of capital equipment, the extension of credit allows for the securing of resources which permit economic advances. But in the plantation context the credit system rarely worked in this way. Most often it simply was a means of containment. This containment was achieved in three ways. First, in the planter/tenant relationship all records were kept by the planter. As a result, the latter was under a constant temptation to manipulate records to his own benefit. Though the extent of cheating is impossible to document, one suspects that the amount of money which was involved represented greater than trivial amounts.* Second, because the planter was the sole source of credit, he was in the position of a monopolist. According to economic theory, then, credit was both less available and more expensive to the tenant than would have been the case under more competitive circumstances. Finally, credit was made available only for retail purchases, meaning that the credit system was of little assistance to tenants attempting to mobilize resources for investment purposes.

The combined result was that the credit which was available, whether offered at rates which were usurious or not, certainly was not cheap. Above and beyond that formal rate, many tenants were required to pay a "cheating premium." The availability of credit was restricted both with respect to its quantity and the use to which it could be put. When contrasted to a hypothetical, more competitive and unrestricted system, therefore, the severe limitations of the plantation credit system are obvious. In short, the control and allocation of credit were principal manifestations of the unilateral power relationships characteristic of plantation life and in turn further reinforced these relationships.

Thus, close observation of the region where plantations existed in large numbers as late as 1910 tends to confirm that there did indeed exist a plantation economy in at least parts of the deep South. In the 325 counties identified by the Census Bureau as plantation counties, sharecropping was the principal means by which the estates obtained their labor force and there was almost total concentration in the production of cotton. In these counties compared to nonplantation counties there was a disproportionate

---

*This story, though probably apocryphal, illustrates the point. A tenant offering five bales of cotton was told, after some owl-eyed figuring, that his cotton exactly balanced his debt. Delighted at the prospect of a profit this year, the tenant reported that he had one more bale which he hadn't brought in. "Shucks," shouted the boss, "why didn't you tell me before? Now I'll have to figure the account all over again to make it come out even."[17]

number of blacks, but at the same time black land ownership was inordinately low. Finally, the estates were under the close supervision of the planters who, through a variety of means, dominated life and decision-making on the plantations.

V. TECHNOLOGICAL CHANGE AND DEVELOPMENT

In his Nobel Prize address, Simon Kuznets defined modern economic growth as a long-term rise in the capacity to supply increasingly diverse goods. This enhanced capacity, he went on, was "based on advancing technology and the institutional and ideological adjustments that it demands." Advancing technology, for Kuznets,

. . . is the *permissive* source of economic growth, but it is only a potential, a necessary condition, in itself, not sufficient. For any level of technology to be used efficiently and for new technology to be stimulated, institutional and ideological adjustments must be made.[1]

Thus, where economic growth is present, its proximate cause is improving technology; but lying behind these advances were facilitating institutional and ideological changes. Such a view of the process of modern economic growth is not inconsistent with a Marxist approach to the study of growth and development. For Marxists accept the centrality of technological change in the process. What Marxists do, in addition, however, is to attempt to specify the institutional and ideological circumstances in which technological change occurs, a specification process which Kuznets largely skips over.

Marxists believe that capitalist relations of production have historically been the institutional framework best suited to the development of modern technology. These relations were at once called into existence by the embryonic development of new forces of production and accelerated the rate at which technological change occurred. By contrast, noncapitalist relations of production acted to constrain technological advance. As a consequence these had to be dismantled in order to facilitate technological advance. Thus Marx and Engels wrote in the *Communist Manifesto* that conservation of the old mode of production in unaltered form was

... the first condition of existence of all earlier industrial classes [while] constant revolutionizing of production, uninterrupted disturbance of all social conditions, everlasting uncertainty, and agitation distinguish the bourgeois epoch from all earlier ones.[2]

The Marxian hypothesis, then, is that where the capitalist mode of production prevails, technological change and therefore economic development will be more rapid than where a different institutional framework is present. This thesis is especially pertinent in our context, where the argument precisely is that a nonbourgeois mode of production continued to exist in the postbellum South even after the Civil War. Specifically we would want to know whether the structure of the plantation economy retarded economic development in the South.

As we have seen the region of the South which concerns us, the plantation South, specialized in the production of cotton. Assuming that this specialization followed from a comparative advantage which the region experienced in this crop as a result of soil and particularly climatic conditions, a first step which would be necessary to test the Marxian hypothesis would be to compare the productivity experience of cotton with other comparable staples grown in nonplantation economies. Evidence that productivity in cotton grew more slowly than in the other crops would stand as supportive evidence for the Marxian view that noncapitalist plantation relations of production impeded economic development. Evidence to the contrary would tend to contradict the Marxian hypothesis. In either case, however, further analysis would be needed to ascertain the precise mechanisms by which any such differentials were generated.

In this chapter we attempt to do two things: (1) examine the data to determine the extent to which they support or contradict the hypothesis that the plantation economy inhibited economic development and (2) attempt to account for the patterns observed.

The U. S. Department of Agriculture has prepared estimates of the man-hour requirements which were necessary to produce

500 pound bales of cotton and 100 bushels of wheat and corn over a period dating from 1840 to 1920. A decrease in these measures indicates an increase in labor productivity and stands as a proxy for technological change. By comparing the performance of cotton on the one hand and wheat and corn on the other, we are able to provide an initial test of the hypothesis that the structure of the plantation economy inhibited the process of technological advance.

In Table V.1 the percentage declines achieved in these man-hour requirements are calculated. They provide an initial confirmation of our hypothesis. Over the entire period the advance in labor productivity in cotton was less than half that in wheat and only about 60 percent of that in corn. Furthermore, the relatively poor performance in cotton is observed in each of the time periods for which we have data, though the experience was least bad for the 1840–1880 period.

These results, however, are themselves a function of changes in two other variables: changes in man-hour requirements per acre and changes in yields per acre. A decrease in man-hour requirements per acre, assuming yields to be constant, would show up as a decrease in man-hours per unit of output. The same would be the case were there an increase in yields, holding man-hour per-acre requirements constant. Thus movements in labor productivity are determined by movements in land productivity or yields and man-hour requirements per acre, a proxy for farm mechanization. Changes in these two are reported in Tables V.2 and V.3, while the contribution of each separately to the overall increase in labor productivity is reported in Table V.4.

The principal conclusions which seem to emerge from Tables V.1 to V.4 are these:

1. The rate of labor productivity advance during the period 1840–1920 was slower in cotton than in the other two commodities. The slow growth of labor productivity in cotton was particularly marked in the period 1900–1920 (Table V.1).

2. The principal determinant of the rate of productivity advance for all three crops was mechanization. In only one instance did the movement in yields outweigh the movement associated with mechanization in influencing changes in labor productivity

TABLE V.1. Percentage Decrease in Man-Hours Required per 100 Bushels of Wheat and Corn and 500-Pound Bales of Cotton: 1840–1920

Year	Wheat	Corn	Cotton
1840–1880	34.8	34.8	30.8
1880–1900	28.9	18.3	6.9
1900–1920	19.4	23.1	0.7
1840–1920	62.7	59.1	36.0

SOURCE: Calculated from Martin R. Cooper, Glen T. Barton and Albert P. Brodell, *Progress of Farm Mechanization*, U.S. Department of Agriculture, Miscellaneous Publications No. 630, Table 1.

(Table V.4). Thus the slow growth in labor productivity in cotton can be attributed to the fact that the process of mechanization in this crop was slower than in the others. Direct confirmation of this is provided in Table V.2.

3. The sharp advance in labor productivity in cotton which did occur between 1840 and 1880 was the one instance in which changes in yields out-weighed changes in mechanization (Tables V.3 and V.4). In this case it is probable that increasing yields are associated with the westward movement of the locus of cotton cultivation. On the other hand, the period in which mechanization proceeded most rapidly, in cotton 1900–1920 (Table V.2), did not see a substantial rise in labor productivity because during these years yields in cotton declined sharply, a decline probably accounted for by the boll weevil infestation which occurred in these years (Tables V.3 and V.4).

The period 1840–1920 was therefore one in which cotton lagged behind the other crops with regard to labor productivity and mechanization. By the end of the period the process of mechani-

TABLE V.2. Percentage Decrease Man-Hours per Acre of Wheat, Corn and Cotton: 1840–1920

Year	Wheat	Corn	Cotton
1840–1880	42.9	33.3	11.9
1880–1900	25.0	17.4	5.9
1900–1920	20.0	15.8	19.6
1840–1920	65.7	53.6	33.3

SOURCE: Table V.1.

TABLE V.3.   Percentage Change in Bushels per Acre of Wheat and Corn and
Pounds of Gross Cotton Lint per Acre: 1840–1920

Year	Wheat	Corn	Cotton
1840–1880	−12.0	+2.4	+27.3
1880–1900	+5.3	+1.2	+0.1
1900–1920	+0.1	+9.7	−19.2
1840–1920	−8.0	+13.6	+3.8

SOURCE: Table V.1.

zation in cotton had accelerated, a process which failed to show
up in increased labor productivity only because of an exogenous
factor affecting yields.

At least partial confirmation of the impression that cotton lagged
behind the other crops in mechanization throughout the nineteenth century is provided in Jacob Schmookler's data on patent
grants. Schmookler collected data on the number of patents
granted by commodity and process, letting these time series
stand as a proxy for levels of inventive activity and technological
change. In this case his data are confined to the harvesting of
cotton, corn, and grain. They demonstrate a similar trend by crop
as is reported in the Department of Agriculture's estimates of
productivity change. As is seen in Table V.5, over the entire period annual patent activity in cotton was lower than for the other
two crops, but by the twentieth century this shortfall had been

TABLE V.4.   Percentage Contribution of Mechanization to Decreasing Man-
Hour Requirements per 100 Bushels of Corn and Wheat and 500-Pound Bales
of Cotton

Year	Wheat	Corn	Cotton
1840–1880	124.7	95.8	38.5
1880–1900	86.4	95.7	90.5
1900–1920	102.0	70.6	285.0
1840–1920	105.3	90.8	92.7

SOURCE: Table V.1. Calculated by assuming yields remained constant over the relevant
years, but using actual decrease in man-hour requirements per acre for these same years
and calculating percentage of total decrease in man-hour requirements per unit of output
contributed by the latter.

TABLE V.5. Average Annual Number of Patents Granted for Grain and Corn Harvesting, Threshing and Cutting and Cotton Harvesting, Picking and Chopping Plows: 1837/1859—1900/1919

Year	Grain	Corn	Cotton
1837–1859	10.3	12.4	1.2
1860–1879	35.4	34.2	11.1
1889–1899	57.2	48.7	25.9
1900–1919	47.1	63.0	46.1
1837–1919	35.9	37.8	20.5

SOURCE: Jacob Schmookler, *Patents, Inventions and Economic Change, Data and Selected Essays*, edited by Zvi Griliches and Leonid Hurwicz (Cambridge: Harvard University Press, 1972), pp. 100-103.

narrowed when cotton was compared to corn and eliminated when cotton was compared to grain.

Overall, then, the evidence presented here indicates that at least during the nineteenth century, mechanization and inventive activity proceeded at a slower pace in cotton than in other major agricultural staples. These data on agricultural productivity tend to suggest that technological change was slower in those parts of the country characterized by plantation agriculture than elsewhere, especially before the beginning of the twentieth century.

There is, in addition to these data on the cotton experience, evidence that, even within the South, the process of economic growth generally was less successful in the plantation regions than in the nonplantation areas.[3] To look at this possibility we compared the experience of the six states in which plantation agriculture was most important with seven nonplantation southern states with respect to three variables closely associated with the development experience. Trends in per capita income are a single, more-or-less direct measure of economic growth; trends in the percentage of the labor force in agriculture indicate the degree of economic diversification experienced; and trends in illiteracy and school attendance tap the educational experience, a variable closely associated with economic development.

Unfortunately, state income estimates apparently have not been prepared for 1860, making it impossible to compare the experience of the plantation states with the nonplantation southern

TABLE V.6.   Total Income per Capita and Percentage Change by State: 1880–1900

State	Total Income per Capita		% Change
	1800	1900	
Alabama	56	62	10.7
Arkansas	62	63	1.6
Georgia	56	56	0.0
Louisiana	69	73	5.8
Mississippi	64	62	−3.1
South Carolina	51	57	11.8
Weighted Mean[a]	59	62	.5.1
Virginia	51	66	29.4
West Virginia	54	79	46.3
North Carolina	46	54	17.4
Florida	48	67	39.6
Kentucky	58	69	19.0
Tennessee	52	61	17.3
Texas	60	84	40.0
Weighted Mean[a]	53	69	30.2

[a]Weighted by 1900 population.
SOURCE: Richard A. Easterlin, "Interregional Differences in per Capita Income, Population, and Total Income, 1840–1950" in *Trends in the American Economy—The Nineteenth Century*, Vol. 24, Studies in Income and Wealth (Princeton: Princeton University Press, 1960), Appendix A.

states for either 1840–1860 or 1860–1880. Such a comparison can be made, however, for the 1880–1900 period and is presented in Table V.6. The evidence reported here suggests that the plantation states did indeed grow more slowly than the nonplantation states. During these years the rate of growth of the slowest-growing nonplantation state exceeded that of the most rapidly growing plantation state. The average percentage increase for the seven nonplantation states was almost six times that of the plantation states with the weighted mean for the latter 5.1 compared to 30.2 for the former.

Table V.7 presents data on the percentage of the labor force employed in agriculture for the six plantation states and the other

TABLE V.7. Agricultural Labor Force as Percentage of Total Labor Force, by State: 1870–1910

State	1870	1880	1890	1900	1910
Alabama	82.0	83.4	72.3	71.2	66.4
Arkansas	82.2	85.6	76.7	74.6	69.3
Georgia	78.3	78.3	64.8	64.5	62.1
Louisiana	61.5	67.3	63.0	61.5	49.4
Mississippi	85.6	86.0	80.7	80.0	76.4
South Carolina	81.8	81.3	77.0	73.4	70.1
Weighted mean[a]	78.8	80.4	72.0	70.5	65.4
Virginia	64.0	61.0	51.3	50.7	43.9
West Virginia	67.9	67.4	57.2	51.9	35.7
North Carolina	80.1	78.9	71.7	68.9	63.5
Florida	75.1	70.8	52.4	45.3	36.6
Kentucky	67.5	67.4	58.1	58.8	52.2
Tennessee	76.2	73.4	63.2	61.8	54.3
Texas	74.9	75.8	65.8	67.4	59.6
Weighted Mean[a]	72.0	71.8	61.3	60.6	52.8

[a]Weighted by population at each census year.

SOURCE: Simon Kuznets, Ann Ratner Miller, and Richard A. Easterlin, *Population Redistribution and Economic Growth, United States, 1870–1950*, Vol. II, Analysis of Economic Change, Table A2.4, p.82.

southern states for the years 1870–1910. These data also tend to confirm the plantation retardation thesis since they indicate that the shift of labor out of agriculture was slower in the states in which plantation agriculture was important compared to the other southern states.

For all observations between 1870 and 1910 the share of the labor force in agriculture is greater in the plantation states than in the others. Over time the percentage in agriculture in both sets of states declined, but the rate of decline was greater in the nonplantation states than in the plantation states. In 1870 the ratio of the plantation to nonplantation percentage of the labor force in agriculture stood at 109.4; by 1910 this ratio was 123.9.

Generally, there was about a twenty-year lag in the plantation states compared to the others with respect to the declining per-

centage of workers in agriculture. Thus, it was not until 1890 that
the proportion of agricultural workers in the plantation states was
equal to that of the other southern states in 1870. However, in
1910 the plantation states' agricultural labor force still had not
declined to the 1890 level for the nonplantation states.

Finally, we examine census data on education to test the
hypothesis that the plantation states lagged behind the other
southern states in this index of development and modernization
as well. We compute two indices of education: first, the illiteracy
rate and, second, the percentage of the school age population
attending classes (Table V.8). Slight changes in census definitions
may tend to impair the comparability of these data over time.
Nonetheless the pattern is clear. Measured in either way, educational achievement in the plantation South lagged behind the
rest of the region. As late as 1900 the illiteracy rate stood at 20.0
percent compared to 11.7 percent for the other southern states,
while school attendance rates also were inferior in the plantation
states throughout the period. Thus, in this regard as well as the
others mentioned above, the plantation states stood at a relatively
inferior position compared to the nonplantation South through
much of the nineteenth century.

Why did cotton lag behind wheat and corn in the pace of technological change? Why did the southern plantation states lag
behind the southern nonplantation states with regard to important
indices of economic development? In this section we address
these issues. Unfortunately the answers we develop will only be
imperfect and far from the last word on this subject. For as yet
there is no fully articulated theory of economic development
from which we can derive an exhaustive set of hypotheses to
analyze the reasons for the relatively unfavorable experience
which occurred in the region which concerns us.

Recent work in explaining differential rates of technological
advance has used a framework which sees such achievements as
a form of economic behavior whose level is explainable through
the use of economic reasoning. In particular this means that the
hypotheses which are developed to account for differences by
product or region in the rate of technological change center on

TABLE V.8 Percentage Illiterate and Percentage of School Age Population Attending School, by State: 1860, 1880, 1900.

State	1860		1880		1900	
	Illiterate[a]	School Age Attending School[b]	Illiterate	School Age Attending School[b]	Illiterate	School Age Attending School[b]
Alabama	23.7	25.3	29.3	39.4	21.1	32.8
Arkansas	16.5	24.0	19.1	36.2	11.6	43.5
Georgia	22.7	31.4	39.0	41.1	18.9	35.4
Louisiana	27.4	20.1	31.6	24.1	35.9	28.6
Mississippi	33.6	20.6	27.9	54.8	19.8	40.9
South Carolina	34.3	16.9	32.3	36.4	22.3	68.1
Weighted Mean[c]	26.4	25.0	28.5	38.4	20.0	40.4
Virginia	19.0	25.4	23.8	40.0	14.8	42.8
West Virginia	N.A.	N.A.	8.4	61.7	6.1	52.3
North Carolina	21.2	29.9	26.3	49.9	16.7	42.1
Florida	23.4	15.4	26.1	43.5	13.8	44.0
Kentucky	14.0	40.3	15.7	47.1	10.0	48.3
Tennessee	16.6	36.7	19.1	50.0	12.2	43.7
Texas	14.0	27.3	16.1	30.1	9.0	42.4
Weighted Mean[c]	17.3	31.9	19.6	45.1	11.7	44.5

[a]Slaves over 20 in 1860 are assumed to be illiterate and not attending school.
[b]School age is 5–19 inclusive in 1860 and 1880 and 5–20 inclusive in 1900.
[c]Weighted by population at each census year.

SOURCES: United States Census: 1900: Vol. 1, Population; 1880: Vol. 1, Population, pt. 1,2; 1860: Vol. 1, Population.

the cost of engaging in inventive activity or introducing new methods of production compared to the benefits which are received from such activity. Differences among the suggested explanations show up with regard to the factors held dominant in raising or lowering the cost of the process of innovation. In general, a line can be drawn between those hypotheses which emphasize the degree of difficulty and feasibility which exists in achieving productivity advances and the degree of incentive which exists to engage in technological advance. Hypotheses in the first class can be referred to as supply hypotheses and those in the second class can be referred to as demand hypotheses.

Recently, for example, Nathan Rosenberg has emphasized the need to pay careful attention to supply side considerations in discussing technological change. Rosenberg writes that inventions are not equally possible in all industries because of different levels of scientific development at any point in time. Rosenberg's view is that with the development of scientific knowledge ". . . the cost of successfully undertaking any given science-based invention declines."[4] Science thus underlies the supply function of inventions and technological advance. Advances in the stock of knowledge are treated as resulting in a rightward shift in the supply function of new inventions. Thus the more knowledge, the lower the cost of invention and the greater the number of inventions and technological breakthroughs which will come to fruition. The industries for which science has progressed most, then, will be those in which the supply function is most to the right. Assuming the demand for inventions is equal over all industries, it follows that the ones which will experience the most rapid rates of productivity advance are those in which the stock of knowledge is greatest. Conversely, in those in which science has progressed least, there will be only limited technological advance. According to this hypothesis, then, all industries are searching for cost-reducing technological changes, but those best able to secure such advantages will be those where prior scientific breakthroughs set the stage for productivity growth.

Applied to the case of cotton this hypothesis would suggest that the relatively slow pace of technological change in cotton might have resulted from the difficulty of the technical problems encountered with that crop. It would suggest that the scientific breakthroughs necessary to achieve successes were more substantial than in other crops and it was this which produced the lag in the rate of technological advance in cotton. There is some evidence that technical difficulties, particularly in the harvesting of cotton, were more difficult than in the other crops. As we shall see, however, it does not seem likely that these were the principal sources of the slow pace of technological change in the industry.

James H. Street lists four complicating factors which made difficult the mechanizing of the cotton harvest. First was the fact that soil types varied, with the result that machinery suited to some circumstances was unworkable in others. Differences in the genetic characteristics of the cotton plant and variations in cultivation practices similarly made the adoption of a mass-produced harvester difficult. These, however, appear to be unlikely sources of a long-term or a considerable lag in technology. This is so since, as Street points out, such problems might have affected a mass-marketed harvester, but still would have permitted the development of a set of machines each suited to local conditions.[5]

A potentially more serious problem was the fact that bolls on the cotton plant do not ripen at a uniform rate. This means that a method of harvest is required which strips the plant of the ripened bolls, but leaves intact and uninjured the unripened bolls. With handpicking this problem means that pickers went over the same crop three or four times. The same repetition was required of a mechanized picker, with the added complication that the machine be selective and not damage unripened bolls.

Notwithstanding this problem, Street, the principal historian of cotton technology, argues that these technical difficulties were not the principal reasons that technology lagged in cotton.[6] In this connection Schmookler's patent data seem to support Street's skepticism. For what the patent data indicate are efforts to find solutions, not the viability of the solutions themselves. Seen from this perspective, what is significant about cotton is that so few efforts were made to solve the technical problems, not that the technical problems remained unsolved at a relatively later date.

The difficulties encountered in the harvesting of cotton were mechanical. They did not require the application of new scientific principles, only the solving of the physical problem of not injuring the cotton plant while stripping it of the fiber. The fact that relatively few patents were granted in cotton suggests that efforts made in this area were few. It was this limited effort which was the key to the delay in achieving a mechanical breakthrough. Furthermore, in principle, the problem of leaving undamaged, unripened cotton bolls was not different from that faced in corn where there was a need to separate the ear from the stalk, while preserving the stalk for forage.[7] It thus appears unlikely that technological supply considerations—emphasizing the level of theoretical science and technology—adequately account for the lagging technological advance experienced in cotton.

On the demand side, two different explanations have been offered to explain why entrepreneurs in some industries might have a greater incentive to adopt new techniques than businessmen in other industries. One of these arguments is associated with the work of Jacob Schmookler. Schmookler attempted to account for variations in inventive activity over time by focusing on the incentive to engage in this kind of behavior—a demand side explanation. The incentive identified by Schmookler is associated with the sale of capital goods to a particular industry. Schmookler's view was that the expected gain from inventive activity "varies with the expected sale of improved capital goods embodying the inventions and [that] expected sales of improved capital goods are largely determined by present capital goods sales."[8] Thus the higher the level of capital goods sales, the greater the anticipated potential returns from inventive activity and hence the greater the incentive to engage in that form of economic activity. In turn, the demand for capital goods by an industry is a positive function of the demand for the commodity itself produced in the industry. Thus, a full statement of the line of causality suggested by Schmookler points to an increased demand for the final product augmenting the demand for intermediate capital goods, and this, in turn, triggers increased inventive activity and technological advance.

Schmookler's demand hypothesis would find confirmation where a relatively slow growth in productivity is associated with a weak market performance. Such an experience might lead to lower levels of investment and thus lower rates of technological change than for a crop with a relatively strong market performance. Thus a fairly simple test of the Schmookler hypothesis with regard to the lag in productivity in cotton would be to compare the market for it with the market for the other two crops considered in this chapter—wheat and corn.

In Table V.9 we compare the price and output experience of wheat, corn, and cotton between 1881–1885 and 1906–1910. These years were selected so as to avoid those immediately after the Civil War. If the latter had been included, they would have shown an even larger increase in market prices than appear in this table. But to do so would have been to exaggerate the strength of the cotton market since for much of this period southern cotton was merely reestablishing its position in the market and not responding to new market opportunities.

Line 1 shows that, over the period, the production of cotton grew more rapidly than was the case for corn or wheat. But Line 2 indicates that, while this was occurring, the price of cotton rose, an increase comparable to that of corn and superior to that of wheat which held about constant. Increases in price occurring at the same time that output is advancing suggests that the demand for the product was increasing even more than was supply. These data thus suggest that the market for cotton was stronger than for either of the two other crops. That cotton output increased much more than corn and yet their price trends were similar suggests a

TABLE V.9. Percentage Changes in Production and Prices—Corn, Wheat, Cotton: 1881/1885–1906/1910

	Corn	Wheat	Cotton
Production	+58.0	+40.1	+95.1
Price	+21.6	+0.6	+17.1

SOURCE: *Historical Statistics of the United States, Colonial Times to 1957*, Series K265-73 and K298-306 (Washington: Government Printing Office, 1960).

more favorable shift in demand for cotton than corn. Similarly, the superior experience of cotton in both production and price indicates the presence of a stronger market for cotton than for wheat.

The fact that the cotton market was stronger than the market for corn or wheat is inconsistent with the Schmookler hypothesis. Cotton did experience a lower level of productivity growth than the other two crops, but unlike what would be anticipated following Schmookler's line of reasoning, this relatively poor performance in productivity was not associated with a weaker product market.

In contrast to the demand argument offered by Schmookler which emphasizes the importance of the product market, a second demand framework has been offered which points to the central importance of the input markets, and specifically the labor market. Nathan Rosenberg's name is associated with this approach too, though he advanced his demand argument some years before he argued for the preeminence of supply conditions. Rosenberg argued then as he does in the article cited above, that the prior level of scientific development is itself an important variable in looking at new technological advances. But in this earlier article Rosenberg attempts to identify "inducement mechanisms," to achieve such breakthroughs.

In reviewing a series of historic episodes the outcome of which were advances in technique, Rosenberg identified three circumstances in which there emerged a compelling demand for new methods of production. First, he cites several instances in which a technical imbalance between interdependent processes in production led to pressure to introduce technical advance. Bottlenecks to more efficient production caused by a lagging technology in one stage of production set up an enhanced incentive to achieve breakthroughs in that backward sector. A second mechanism inducing technological change was centered on the availability and reliability of labor. Rosenberg argues that in England at the time of the industrial revolution, "The apparent recalcitrance of . . . labor, especially skilled labor, in accepting the discipline and the terms of factory employment, provided an inducement to technical change." The limited supply of such labor and/or the threat of strikes focused the attention of decision-makers on the resulting threat to their profits from this source and spurred business people to achieve changes in methods of production involving either less skilled or fewer workers. Finally Rosenberg argues that disruptions in normal patterns of supply also stimulate the search for new methods of production and new products. In particular, war is identified as a stimulant for technological change in this way.[9]

The common denominator running through Rosenberg's three focusing devices—technical imbalance, the threat of labor shortages, and supply disruptions—is the fact that they focused the attention of entrepreneurs on the "most restrictive constraint on their operations." That such attention yielded new techniques presumes the adequacy of the underlying stock of knowledge to achieve such advances. But the direction and extent of the search for such techniques in this model depend upon inducement mechanisms and focusing devices relating to the demand for advances in productivity. According to this hypothesis, advances in production methods occur when a firm is faced with a production problem that identifies the need for a technological breakthrough. This acts to produce an increased demand for such an innovation. If technically feasible, the result is an enhanced likelihood of a development of new methods of production.

It appears that this same logic can be used to offer an hypothesis to account for an absence or retardation in technological change. The argument would be that assuming the existence in two products of an equal supply of relevant knowledge and engineering know-how, the product with the slower advance in productivity would be the one in which focusing devices were least present. Where supply factors, in short, are held constant, a slow rate of technological change can be traced to the existence of only a limited incentive to introduce new techniques. In the case of cotton specifically this would suggest the hypothesis that, in the cultivation of this crop compared to wheat and corn, attention was less devoted to the need to change production methods because it confronted production disruptions less frequently.

This hypothesis is, of course, quite consistent with the actual experience in cotton. For the plantation economy was organized precisely to avoid production disruptions, especially with regard to labor availability. All of the repressive mechanisms of the plantation economy performed the function of ensuring the continuous availability of unskilled labor to the estates in large numbers. To the extent that these instruments succeeded in allowing for the viability of the plantation economy, they also meant that the demand for productivity advances was less than would have been the case in their absence, and therefore less than was the case in the less repressive circumstances associated with the cultivation of wheat and corn.

The functioning of the coercive institutions of the plantation economy reduced the incentive to engage in technological change in cotton. So, too, did the cost and relative unavailability of capital funds. Lance Davis has analyzed how in the evolution of a national capital market in the United States between 1870 and 1914, "the South stood apart." Neither long- nor short-term markets effectively developed in the region. Interest rates in the South were considerably higher than elsewhere, with relatively few banks present. What accounted for the differential experience by region in the evolution of capital markets is not yet clear. Davis, for example, concludes that "the question of why the South lagged is still open."[10]

What is clear is that these conditions tended to reduce the rate of productivity advance. The fact of the undeveloped state of the capital market in the South tended to make credit both more expensive and less available than it would have been if the markets in that region had been as well developed as those elsewhere. This high price of capital in association with the relatively low cost of labor (see Table VI.2) provided a disincentive for management to substitute capital for labor in the production process. But to the extent that technological change is embodied in new machinery, precisely this deterrent would produce a relatively lower rate of productivity advance than if factor prices had been such as to encourage an increase in capital intensity in production.[11]

What all of this meant was that cotton planters had less incentive to search for and implement new methods of production than did farmers elsewhere in the United States. Planters were faced with fewer profit-threatening disruptions than existed in parts of the country where a wider range of occupational alternatives was available. Furthermore, credit essential to the financing of major technical innovations was both more expensive and less available than in other parts of the country. Planters were thus more content with existing production methods than they would have been if a focusing device had been present or if they had been given price signals through the capital market to increase the relative extent to which they employed machinery in production. This is not to say that no search for profit-increasing improvements was undertaken. Nor is it to argue that there were not important conceptual breakthroughs necessary before a viable harvester could be marketed. Rather, the argument is that the urgency to achieve such a breakthrough was less in the situation of the southern plantation economy than would have been the case in different institutional circumstances.

The plantation economy functioned to provide large numbers of cheap workers to estates employing a labor-intensive technology. Various mechanisms such as racial discrimination and paternalism were operative to secure this result. These techniques were successful and large-scale, labor-intensive cotton production was thereby made profitable. In the process, however, the very success achieved in maintaining the viability of plantation agriculture served in its turn to reduce the incentive to change production methods on the estates. The relative inability of blacks to find alternative employment opportunities tended to produce a technological conservatism in the plantation economy which would have been less marked if escape from plantation labor had been a real option for large numbers of blacks. Such opportunities would have raised plantation labor costs and reduced the labor supply available to the estates, both tending to produce a more rapid rate of technological change. It was, then, the very mechanism which supported plantation agriculture that in addition tended to induce technological stagnation in production methods.

The structure of the plantation economy was initially a response to a serious constraint to profitable production: labor-intensive technology in an environment in which labor was scarce. Institutional arrangements were devised to by-pass a free labor market and provide workers in large numbers and at low costs to the producing units. The argument of this chapter is that there was a feedback process from these institutional arrangements and that the same institutions which allowed for the profitable use of labor-intensive technologies tended to freeze the technological capacity of the southern society at that relatively primitive level. Behaving in a manner which economists consider rational, southern planters refrained from shifting to more capital-intensive but also more expensive "advanced" production methods. The decision not to search for new production methods at once is testimony to the profit-maximizing behavior of the planters and to the efficacy of the check on black labor's search for alternative employment opportunities. The evidence adduced in this chapter thus supports the hypothesis that the plantation economy was a considerably less favorable mode of production for the adoption and spread of new technology than was a capitalist economy.

VI. MIGRATION NORTH

The South experienced a substantial degree of socioeconomic continuity between the pre- and post-Civil War periods. The black population was at once trapped by and continued to provide the manpower base for the South's plantation economy. The terms of that entrapment and the ideology reinforcing that imprisonment had been altered, but the essentials of the plantation economy had successfully survived slave emancipation.

But while there was continuity, the failure of the "War for Southern Independence"[1] had resolved one basic issue: the plantation South was to be only a subordinate part of a generally more dynamic capitalist economy and was not going to be permitted to chart its own independent course. In short, the South was still a part of a union dominated by a ruling class rooted elsewhere than in plantation agriculture. This duality—that the plantation South was different from, but part of, the capitalist United States—was decisive with regard to the ultimate fates of both the southern plantations and their workers.

Interindustry and interregional immobility had been an important prop to the South's plantation economy. But this rigidity was antagonistic both to the economic needs and dominant ideology of the rest of the country. Indeed, labor mobility, the movement of workers from relatively low-productivity work to occupations where their productivity was higher provided an important source of economic growth in the American experience.[2] Furthermore the dominant *laissez-faire* ideology characteristic of the northern society approved and reinforced the view that "factors of production" such as labor should be free to search out and secure jobs yielding higher rates of pay without interference, particularly without official governmental intervention.

But pressures from outside the South to end the system of coercion remained weak as long as the control of manpower in that region did not act as a serious constraint on the profitability of business in the rest of the country. In fact, at least until World

War I, the entrapment of blacks in the South did not retard growth elsewhere; primarily this was because of the ready availability of an alternative source of labor, international migrants. Between 1870 and 1920 immigration to the United States averaged in excess of 500,000 per year, or almost seven immigrants per 1,000 of the population annually.

The mere citing of these data, however, fails to answer the question mentioned earlier of why were largely non-English-speaking Europeans preferred to southern blacks for the emerging northern industrial occupations. Seen from the viewpoint of the prospective employers, such alternative sources of labor might have provided equally acceptable sources of manpower. But the absence of a large interregional movement while a vast international migration was occurring makes it quite clear the preference went to the Europeans. As we have seen in Chapter II it appears that a presumptive case can be made that it was management's racism which was at the bottom of this pattern of demand.

Under these circumstances there was little need for black labor outside of the South. The plantation economy, based as it was on the availability of cheap labor in large numbers, therefore was able to remain intact. Until World War I, the combination of controls internal to the plantation economy and the weak demand for black labor elsewhere in the United States perpetuated the plantation economy and fixed the position of the black population within that structure.

World War I, however, marked the beginning of the end of this situation. Prior to that time, the post-bellum southern plantation economy had rested on a rather delicate equilibrium in which the "external" demand for labor had not overwhelmed the "internal" control of manpower. But that balance was disrupted during World War I when international migration was seriously curtailed. In the absence of new immigrant workers, northern firms flooded the South with recruiters seeking to hire blacks. According to one authority, the Pennsylvania Railroad alone brought 12,000 blacks north to maintain track and equipment, and another estimate has it that 50,000 blacks arrived in Chicago in an eighteen-month period in 1917–1918.[3]

Figure VI.1 illustrates the relationship between international migration to the United States and the movement of blacks from the plantation South. Until the war decade of the 1910s, the rate of migration to the United States remained at high levels, subject only to fluctuations associated with the American business cycle. At the same time very little black outmigration from the South occurred. After 1910, first as a result of the disruption associated with World War I and thereafter because of a set of restrictive laws limiting immigration to the United States, the flow of per-

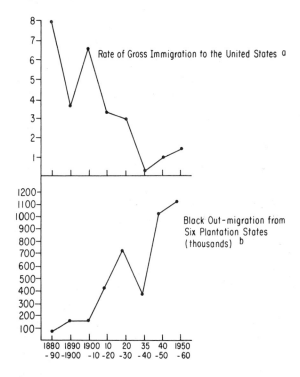

FIGURE VI.1 Rate of Gross Immigration to United States and Black Out-migration from Six Plantation States: 1880/90–1950/60

[a]SOURCE: Lance Davis et al., *American Economic Growth* (New York: Harper & Row, 1972), p. 123.
[b]SOURCE: *Historical Statistics of the United States*, pp. 46–47; and John P. Davis, The American Negro Reference Book, Table 1.

sons into the country was reduced substantially. It was in these years that the movement of blacks from the South experienced an increase. Richard Easterlin has neatly summarized the experience by writing that "with the foreign labor supply largely cut off, periods of high labor demand in the North began increasingly to generate large movements of blacks out of the South."[4]

Since migration rates are estimated using census data, they are available only in decennial periods. This is unfortunate since estimates for the decade of the 1910s masks contrasting experiences: the relatively low rates for the pre-World War I years and the relatively high rates for the years during the war when international migration was sharply reduced. In excess of 350,000 blacks are estimated to have departed from the six plantation states during the 1910s. This figure must have been largely concentrated in the second half of the decade and represents more than a doubling of the number of blacks who left the plantation South in the preceding decade. In the 1920s the rapid pace of out-migration of blacks continued with nearly 700,000 blacks estimated as having vacated the six plantation states in these years.[5]

According to Karl and Alma Taeuber some of the migration rates which were recorded during these years for young Negro males "are almost beyond belief." They cite, for example, the case of Georgia where during the 1920s an incredible 45 percent of black males aged 15-34 in 1920 are estimated to have left the state by 1930. Though no other state experienced quite so high a rate, still the 21.3 percent loss in Alabama and the 14.2 percent loss in Mississippi for this same subgroup of the population indicate that an out-migration of a very large order of magnitude was occurring in this period.[6]

In excess of one million blacks thus migrated from the six plantation states during the two decades of the 1910s and the 1920s. The timing of this movement suggests that it was associated with the "pull" of the demand for labor in the North rather than a "push" mechanism in the South. The boll weevil infestation, a potential source of a "push" of blacks out of the South, had been experienced in Texas in the 1890s and had gradually spread eastward during the early years of the new century. Yet there is little evidence of important population movements—certainly not of the magnitude which occurred after 1915—in association with the spread of this problem. On the other hand, as soon as there was a significant curtailment of international migration to the United States, a movement of blacks out of the South occurred.

Aside from the effects on the migrants themselves, an outward movement of people had potentially disruptive effects on the plantation economy. The chain of causality would run as follows: the outward movement might have created labor scarcities and potential bottlenecks to production, given the labor-intensive technologies in use. These scarcities in their turn might have vested in the labor force uncharacteristic power, both with regard to a probable upward trend in incomes and with regard to social relations where there might have been a decline in the leverage by which planters maintained dominance over the labor force. One possible reaction by the planters to such an increase in labor scarcity, a reimposition of a form of slavery, was, of course, impossible in a setting in which national political power was not possessed by the planter class. The inability to impose a new juridical slavery, combined with increasing costs and declining availability of labor, however, might have threatened not only the paternalism of the plantation economy, but its profits as well. In short, a massive movement north would have confronted the planters with a breakdown of the plantation economy as a way of life.[7]

The disruption in the plantation economy which might have occurred if migration on the scale of the 1920s had continued was delayed because of the Depression of the 1930s. The high rates of unemployment experienced throughout this period symbolized a significant decline in the northern demand for black labor in these years. Whereas the demand for southern black labor had remained high in the 1920s because of the general prosperity experienced in those years and the fact that this demand no longer was satisfied by international migration, now in the 1930s the supply of labor already present in the North exceeded the demand, and as a result market opportunities for blacks narrowed.

The consequence was that South/North migration dropped considerably during this decade compared to the 1920s, with the estimate of migrating blacks from the plantation South down to 340,000.[8]

A sampling of data makes clear the severity of the impact of the Depression on northern blacks. According to the Federal Emergency Relief Administration in 1933 the proportion of urban Negroes on relief stood at 26.7 percent, almost three times the level for urban whites. By city the Urban League learned that in some cases the percentage on relief was even higher. For example, in Cleveland this figure stood at 33 percent, and it was 37 percent in Detroit, and 30 percent in Chicago. A lack of government data on unemployment by race makes it difficult to be more specific than this on the consequences of the Depression, but it seems undoubtedly true, as Mary Ellison has put it, that these relief statistics show "only the tip of the iceberg of the actual amount of destitution."[9]

Thus again in the 1930s, as in earlier periods, conditions outside of the South were permissive of a continuation of the plantation economy. In this case, the Depression and the resultant immiseration of northern urban blacks seems to have slowed the process of black migration sufficiently to allow for continued plantation viability. However, the institutional props supportive of the plantation economy had been severely weakened. All that remained was the control implicit in a weak northern labor market, a control which obviously was contingent upon the continuation of the Depression. That control therefore would be severely compromised upon such time as there was an industrial recovery and a strengthening of the labor market in the North.

The decline in migration from the plantation South in the 1930s compared to the 1920s was substantial and obviously associated with the Depression. It is significant, however, that the level of black migration from this region was comparable during the 1930s to the level reached in the 1910s and larger than any previous decade to that point. The analytic question that arises then is which factor or combination of factors resulted in the continuation of that out-migration from the South, a population flow which remained relatively high despite the virtual collapse of the northern industrial labor market.

One hypothesis which might account for the continuation of migration from the South during the depression of the 1930s would center on the continued sharp disparity in black income levels between the urban North and the plantation South. To test this possibility we examine data on incomes in the plantation economy specifically for the 1930s. These data were collected by the Division of Social Research of the Works Progress Administration in 1934. T. J. Woofter and his associates carried out a survey of 646 plantations concentrated in the six plantation states of Alabama, Arkansas, Georgia, Louisiana, Mississippi and South Carolina, and also included about 30 plantations in North Carolina. Tenant families on these plantations totaled 9,215 or about 14 per plantation. Table VI.1 provides information on the size distribution of the plantations in the sample and indicates that more than half of them were relatively small with less than ten families resident. Only about 10 percent of the estates contained more than 30 families.

Data provided in the survey allow us to estimate income per tenant family on the plantations compared with operator income for each plantation. (See Table VI.2 for the method of estimation.) These estimates reveal a pattern of sharp income inequality and very low levels of income for most participants in the plantation economy. Estimated operator income, for example, was more than ten times the level of income received by tenants. Further-

TABLE VI.1.   Acres in Crops on Plantations: 1934

Total Plantations	Total Acres in Crops	Number of Plantations Specified Acres in Crops						
		Less than 200	200 to 400	400 to 600	600 to 800	800 to 1000	1000 to 1200	1200 to Over
Number, 646	248,513	241	213	81	42	29	15	25
Percentage, 100		37.3	33.0	12.5	6.5	4.5	2.3	3.9

SOURCE: T.J. Woofter, Jr., *Landlord and Tenant on the Cotton Plantations* (Washington: Division of Social Research, Works Programs Administration, 1936), p. 40.

TABLE VI.2   Estimates of Operator and Tenant Net Income: 1934

(1)   Plantation Net Income − Operator Net Income = Tenant Net Income
(2)   Operator Net Income ÷ 645 = Operator Net Income per Plantation
(3)   Tenant Net Income ÷ 645 = Tenant Net Income per Plantation
(4)   Tenant Net Income per Plantation ÷ Tenants per Plantation =
       per Tenant Family Net Income

(1) $3,885,742 − $1,659,082 = $2,226,660
(2) $1,659,082 ÷ 645 = $2,572
(3) $2,226,660 ÷ 645 = $3,452
(4) $3,452 ÷ 14.3 = $241

SOURCE: T. J. Woofter, Jr., *Landlord and Tenant on the Cotton Plantations* (Washington: Division of Social Research, Works Programs Administration, 1936), pp. 69, 77 and 78.

more, as revealed in Table VI.3, at least 60 percent of sharecropper income was received on a non-cash basis in the form of subsistence advances and home use production. Thus these 1934 data reveal that sharecropper annual family income received on a cash basis came to only about $122.

Obviously, income levels for employed black workers in the urban North were higher than this. For example, the median household income for black families in New York at approximately the same time came to $980. In Chicago the level was $726. Low as these figures were they still meant that the migration

TABLE VI.3.   Source of Sharecropper Income: 1934

Total Net Income	$312
Cash Items	122
Cash after Utility	91
Wages	21
A.A.A.	8
Unshared Sales	2
Non-cash Items	190
Subsistence Advances	85
Home Use Production	105

SOURCE: T.J. Woofter, Jr., *Landlord and Tenant on the Cotton Plantations* (Washington: Division of Social Research, Works Programs Administration, 1936), p. 87.

north promised a substantial increase in incomes, provided, of course, that employment was found.[10]

In the meantime, however, the advantage that the South might have possessed over the North—namely, that at least there were jobs available on the plantations, no matter how low paid they might be—was also disappearing.[11] Particularly important in this regard was the implementation of the New Deal agricultural policies starting with the Agricultural Adjustment Act of 1932 (AAA). Faced in 1932 with the "pathetic price" of 5 cents per pound of cotton and a three-year inventory of the crop, AAA policy was to pay farmers to plow under one-fourth of the cotton crop. By so doing, it was anticipated that prices would rise and inventories decline. The combination of the stronger commodity market which would result from the induced scarcity and the subsidies paid to the farmers to withhold production, it was felt, would substantially improve the income position of the cotton producers.

According to Conrad, however, "the 1933 cotton program was put into effect with such speed that little thought was given to the special problems raised by farm tenancy in the South." Specifically the problems centered on two issues: were the sharecroppers and share tenants to be allowed to enter into contracts with the AAA and participate in the subsidy program; and what protection, if any, was to be provided to croppers displaced because of the withdrawal of acreage from production? Conrad indicates that "with no guidelines, administrators tended to fall easily into the pattern of the southern tenant system." This meant that planters and not tenants received the lion's share of the governmental subsidies.

That tenant evictions were an integral part of the AAA program seems clear. Conrad summarizes the situation in the following way:

About 40 percent of the landlord's acreage lay fallow and yet if he kept the same number of tenants his operating expenses for the year would be almost as great. If he evicted tenants he would not have to support them, he would not have to split government benefit money with them, and he would use the rented acres for his own purposes.[12]

In short, given the market structure created under the AAA program the demand for plantation labor declined.

Thus, in addition to the pull of higher living standards in the North, there was a push of black laborers from the South, the latter a consequence of the decreased demand for labor on the plantations. Indeed it appears likely that during these years the relative strength of one compared to the other may have changed with the push intensifying while the pull may have declined because of mounting northern unemployment. In combination these two forces resulted in the number of black sharecroppers operating in the South declining from 393,000 in 1930 to 299,000 in 1940, while other forms of black tenantry also declined from 306,000 to 208,000 over these same years.[13]

The black migration of the 1910 to 1940 period meant that the demographic composition of the plantation counties studied in Chapter 4 experienced a substantial change, though not as dramatic as the one which was to occur after World War II. Between 1910 and 1930 the absolute number of blacks in these counties actually declined by 3.7 percent. It was only with the slowdown of migration in the 1930s that natural population growth (an excess of births over deaths) produced in 1940 a population approximately at the same level as 1910. In the meantime the white population of these counties had continued a slow but steady growth, so that the proportion of blacks in the population exhibited a steady decline from almost 55 percent in 1910 to about 45 percent in 1940 (Table VI.4).

Comparative data by crop are suggestive of the continued dissimilarity between the plantation economy and agriculture in the

TABLE VI.4. Total and Nonwhite Population of 270 Plantation Counties: 1910–1940

Year	Total Population	Nonwhite Population	% Nonwhite
1910	7,195,600	3,933,627	54.7
1920	7,683,842	3,844,758	50.0
1930	8,256,808	3,789,093	45.9
1940	8,822,938	4,005,465	45.4

SOURCE: U.S. Bureau of the Census, census for each year.

rest of the country. Overall labor productivity in cotton advanced between 1920 and 1940 at a more rapid pace than did corn but more slowly than wheat. However, as revealed in Line 2 of Table VI.5, labor requirements per acre in cotton actually increased in this period. Since this measure represents our proxy for mechanization, it follows, as revealed in Line 4 that none of the increase in productivity experienced in cotton in this period was attributable to mechanization, with the entire increase due to increases in yields per acre.

The cotton experience is in contrast not only to that of wheat and corn in this period, but also to previous patterns in cotton itself. It will be recalled that, although the pace of productivity growth between 1840 and 1920 was slower in cotton than in the other two crops, mechanization was the principal source of the increases which were achieved in cotton, just as mechanization was the principal source of advance in the other two crops. The 1920–1940 experience thus reversed the historical pattern of the relative importance of yields per acre and mechanization. It is clear, therefore, that as late as about 1940 no sustained pattern of mechanization in cotton had as yet appeared, an experience very much at variance with that of other principal crops.

Although these data indicate that the plantation economy persisted during the 1920s and 1930s, several sources of instability were beginning to show themselves. For example, part of the

TABLE VI.5   Sources of Productivity Growth in Cotton, Corn, and Wheat: 1920–1940

	Wheat	Corn	Cotton
1. Decrease in man-hours per 100 bushels of wheat and corn and 500 pound bales of cotton %	46.0	26.5	32.0
2. Decrease in man-hour per acre %	37.5	21.9	−8.9
3. Change in output per acre %	15.2	6.7	37.7
4. Contribution of mechanization to decrease in man-hours per 100 bushels of wheat and corn and 500 pound bales of cotton %	82.5	85.0	−25.6

SOURCE: See Table V.1.

strength of the plantation economy had been that it existed far outside of the mainstream of thought and discussion in the United States. As a consequence the grinding poverty which was so much a part of the economic system was not held up to public scrutiny. During this period, however, the existence of the plantation system was made known to a wide audience as a result of numerous studies carried out by scholars centered at the University of North Carolina, such as Rupert Vance, Charles S. Johnson and T. J. Woofter. Though difficult to estimate, the contributions made by these scholars in educating the American people to conditions in the plantation South and thus making them more receptive to later civil rights efforts seem real and significant. To be sure, the light shed on the plantation economy by these and other scholars did not result in immediate changes. Changes in the plantation economy could be expected only when the principal actors in the southern society mobilized themselves to behave in ways inconsistent with the smooth functioning of the plantation economy.

Thus an even more significant promise of change is to be found in the organizing initiatives undertaken by black farmers themselves in this period. Probably the most important of these organizations was the Southern Tenant Farmers' Union. Organized in 1934 the STFU was multiracial and by 1936 totalled 10,000 black members out of a total membership of 31,000. Supported by both the NAACP and Norman Thomas' Socialist Party, the STFU fought for direct governmental subsidy payments to tenants rather than landlords and also struggled against evictions.[14] In Alabama a sharecropper union was organized with similar goals though perhaps a lesser degree of success. The strength of the commitment to such organization by blacks in the South has recently been revealed in Nate Shaw's oral autobiography. In Shaw's case, it appears that the threat of eviction stirred indignation to the point of heroism. In the act of defending the farm and property of a neighbor, Shaw was arrested, tried, convicted and served ten years in prison.[15] The stirring of collective self-defense which Shaw's story epitomizes signals the rejection of the paternalistic ethos of the South which in forbidding such efforts acted to secure the structure of the plantation economy. Again, the full flowering of this creative rejection would await the birth of the civil rights movement.

Finally, the migration itself shook the plantation economy. Not only did leaving the South affect the individuals who moved, but also those who stayed behind. Escape from the plantation economy was demonstrated to be feasible. If the conditions in the urban North were hardly satisfactory, they nonetheless represented a substantial improvement over plantations. The success of one group of migrating blacks made the movement of the next group easier. By establishing a network of friends and relations which would be supportive of the subsequent migrants, the process of escape was facilitated and reinforced itself. To the extent that the network grew, the props supporting the plantation economy were undermined.

Thus, the period from World War I until 1940 was one in which an incremental chipping away at the structure of the plantation economy occurred. The structure remained intact with the planters continuing to control large numbers of dependent workers in the production of the cotton staple. Below the surface, however, large numbers of southern blacks had learned or were learning the route by which they could escape the plantation economy while others were learning to resist the tyranny of the plantation regime through collective action. All the while the plantation structure was coming under increased scrutiny at least among public officials and in the intellectual community. In short, these years represented a period in which the plantation economy was coming to be seen by increasing numbers of southern blacks and their potential allies elsewhere as an anachronism, the structure of which could be attacked either frontally through organizing efforts or indirectly by migration.

VII. BREAKDOWN OF THE PLANTATION ECONOMY

America's entry into World War II marks the principal point of discontinuity in the black experience in the United States. Until then participation in the southern plantation economy had remained the single most important role played by blacks. From this participation followed the fact that most blacks were southern, rural and poor. Now with the major social mobilization associated with the war, masses of black workers were required either directly or indirectly to support the war effort. This meant first that more than at any time previously, black workers were provided with both the means and the opportunity to escape the southern plantation economy. At the same time the vacating of the estates caused by the war accelerated trends towards mechanization of southern agriculture and the downfall of the plantation economy.

Black migration from the six plantation states during the 1940s totaled in excess of one million, a level almost three times that of the 1930s decade and far greater than the black migration of any previous decade. By any standard this was a movement of people of major importance affecting both the migrants themselves and the recipient and donor regions.

The key to this migration was the change which occurred in the demand for black labor during World War II. The magnitude of this change is indicated by a comparison of the employment pattern of blacks in 1940 with that of 1944. For black men, the shift in the occupational structure was clear and dramatic. While most occupation categories remained essentially stable, the proportion of black men who worked on farms fell from over 41 percent to 28 percent in four years. This shift from agricultural occupations was almost perfectly matched by the increase which occurred in industrial employment (Table VII.1). As a result of the shift to factory work, black men represented 10.1 percent of factory

TABLE VII.1. Percentage Distribution of Blacks by Occupation and Sex: April 1940 and April 1944

Category of workers	Males			Females		
	1940	1944	Change	1940	1944	Change
Farm	41.2	28.0	−13.2	16.0	8.1	−7.9
Industrial	17.0	29.7	+12.7	6.5	18.0	+11.5
Laborers	21.4	20.3	−1.1	0.8	2.0	+1.2
Service	15.3	15.1	−0.2	70.3	62.5	−7.8
Clerical and sales	2.0	3.0	+1.0	1.4	3.9	+2.5
Proprietors, managers, and professionals	3.1	3.7	+0.8	5.0	5.5	+0.5

SOURCE: "War and Post-War Trends—Employment of Negroes," *Monthly Labor Review*, January 1945.

operatives in 1944, an increase from the 5.9 percent which they represented in 1940 (Table VII.2).

A similar but not identical pattern of change occurred with respect to female employment. In this case the decline in farm occupations was matched by a decrease in service (mostly do-

TABLE VII.2 Percentage of Blacks Among Total Employed Workers in Specified Occupational Groups by Sex: April 1940 and April 1944

Category of Workers	Males		Females	
	April 1940	April 1944	April 1940	April 1944
Professional and semi-professional	2.8	3.3	4.5	5.7
Proprietors, managers, and officials	1.1	2.1	2.6	4.8
Clerical	1.6	3.5	0.7	1.6
Sales	1.1	1.5	1.2	1.1
Craftsmen, foremen	2.6	3.6	2.2	5.2
Operatives	5.9	10.1	4.7	8.3
Domestic service	60.2	75.2	46.6	60.9
Protective service	2.4	1.7	3.8	--
Personal service	22.8	31.4	12.7	24.0
Farmers, farm managers	12.4	11.0	30.4	23.8
Farm laborers	21.0	21.1	62.0	21.4
Laborers (excluding farm)	21.0	27.6	13.2	35.6
All Employed	8.6	9.8	13.8	12.9

SOURCE: See Table VII.1.

mestic service) employment. Proportionate increases occurred in all other occupational categories for females, though once again it was an expansion in industrial employment which absorbed the bulk of the workers from the declining categories (Table VII.1). It is of interest to note that, despite the movement of black women out of domestic service employment, black females represented 60.9 percent of all domestic workers in 1944 compared to only 46.6 percent in 1940. This indicates that white females moved out of this category even more rapidly than did black women. However, the shift from the farms by black women was more rapid than that of whites. For example, black females constituted only 21.4 percent of female agricultural workers compared to 62.0 percent in 1940 (Table VII.2). By the same token the share of black females acting as operatives increased from 4.7 percent to 8.3 percent. By 1944 almost 10 percent of all factory positions were filled by blacks (males and females) representing just about a doubling of the black representation in this occupational category.

The importance of the war in producing these rapid changes in the black occupational structure is indicated in Table VII.3. There the data indicate how important the munitions industries were in absorbing black labor. The category "metals, chemicals and rubber" shows the largest increase in black workers, both males and females. These were the categories which included the principal war industries such as iron and steel, machinery, and aircraft and shipbuilding. According to the Bureau of Labor Statistics "the actual number of Negro men in this group increased by well over a quarter of a million between 1940 and 1944, tripling in four years."[1]

The occupational advances achieved by blacks during the war did not come easily or automatically. Robert C. Weaver has detailed how, even in the face of critical labor shortages, discriminatory hiring and promotion practices persisted in major industrial centers. Furthermore the pattern of discrimination also persisted in job and vocational training programs, thus limiting in the short run the availability of black labor for skilled trades. The pressure of demand, however, seriously eroded these racist prac-

TABLE VII.3 Percentage Distribution of Employed Blacks by Industry and Sex: April 1940 and April 1944

Industry	Males		Females	
	April 1940	April 1944	April 1940	April 1944
Agriculture	42.0	29.9	16.1	8.1
Forestry and fishing	0.8	0.5	--	--
Mining	1.8	4.2	--	--
Construction	4.9	.7	0.1	--
Manufacturing	16.2	23.9	3.2	13.4
Metals, chemicals, rubber	5.5	13.1	0.2	7.3
Food, clothing, textiles, leather	2.8	4.7	1.8	3.9
All other manufacturing	7.9	6.1	1.2	2.2
Transportation, communications, public utilities	6.8	10.1	0.2	1.1
Trade	9.9	10.9	4.0	10.5
Finance, insurance, real estate	1.9	1.6	0.8	1.3
Business and repair services	1.7	1.5	0.1	0.1
Domestic and personal services	8.4	6.1	68.6	54.4
Amusement, recreation	1.0	0.4	0.3	0.4
Professional services	2.9	3.2	6.1	7.5
Government	1.7	4.0	0.5	3.2
All Employed Blacks	100.0	100.0	100.0	100.0

SOURCE: See Table VII.1.

tices. Especially, pressure was mounted by the war-pressed Roosevelt Administration to curb discriminatory hiring practices. Similarly, organizational representatives of the black community were quick to point out the hypocrisy of fighting a war in the name of democracy abroad while practicing racism domestically. At times this struggle was also joined by sympathetic unions, especially those in the CIO. Underlying these sources of support for equality in the labor market were, of course, the pressure of

demand and the fact that black labor was essential for the successful prosecution of the war effort. As the war Manpower Commis-
sion put it, "we cannot afford the luxury of thinking in terms of
white men's work. It isn't white men's work we had to do—it's
war work and there's more than enough of it."[2]

The changes which had occurred in the demand for black labor
during the war were apparently widely perceived among black
workers. Thus in a study of postwar migration plans among enlisted men carried out in 1944, Jaffe and Wolfbein found that
twice as many blacks as whites anticipated relocating in a new region of the country.[3] There was a pattern of anticipated movement of blacks from the South to the Northeast and to the West, a
set of expectations which corresponded to regional differences in
job opportunities. It was clear, therefore, that blacks in the labor
force did not anticipate that the war-induced changes in the demand for black labor would be reversed after the war. Rather the
apparent feeling was that alternative employment opportunities
would be available to black workers, allowing them to escape the
low-income agricultural jobs of the plantation South.

This optimism with regard to the postwar demand for black
labor was not universally shared. We have seen that a similar
process of occupational advance had once before been initiated
during World War I and the 1920s only to be aborted with the
coming of the depression of the 1930s. A similar experience was
certainly not beyond the realm of possibility in the 1940s, especially if the widely feared post-World War II economic decline was
permitted to occur. Thus the Bureau of Labor Statistics early
sounded the warning. Noting that blacks had achieved their big-
gest advances "in those industries (especially the 'metals, chemicals and rubber' group) which will experience the greatest post-
war declines" and that, by the rules of seniority, blacks will be the
first to be laid off in these industries, the bureau warned that the
wartime gains might be jeopardized if a contraction in the demand for nonagricultural labor were permitted in the postwar
period. The bureau argued that "the consolidation of the Negro's
gains in the postwar period . . . is dependent in large measure
upon the volume of employment that then prevails."[4] In other

words, the exigencies of war were responsible for the very rapid upgrading of occupations among black workers, but it was yet to be established that these gains were secure in the postwar period.

If the future of black labor in the North remained unclear, the fact of the massive wartime migration of blacks from the South had profound and immediate implications for the plantation economy. It will be recalled that a principal factor militating against labor displacing technological change in cotton had been the availability of abundant, low-cost and dependent labor. This, in combination with the relative scarcity of funds for capital investment in the South, meant that profit-maximizing growers would tend to favor labor-intensive production methods. In turn this meant that the labor force itself experienced low levels of productivity since it was not provided with sufficient complementary tools and equipment to secure high levels of output per worker.

This situation was fundamentally reversed with the migration of the World War II period. It is not possible to estimate precisely the magnitude of the shift which occurred in the supply function of labor, though it is apparent that it was quite dramatic. James Street has calculated that between 1940 and 1945 there was a 20.6 percent decline in the farm populations of South Carolina, Georgia and Alabama and a 23.1 percent decline in Mississippi, Arkansas and Louisiana.[5] Evidence of markedly increasing wage rates during this period makes it appear unlikely in the extreme that these declines were primarily due to a fall in the demand for labor. The magnitude of these increased costs is suggested by the fact that the U. S. Department of Labor reported in 1946 that the price of laborers for cotton picking stood at 7 cents a pound, up from a level of about 1 cent a pound which had prevailed during the 1930s.[6] As a result it seems reasonable to assume that it was this movement of the population which was responsible for a leftward shift in the supply function of labor and which resulted in the dramatic upward movement in farm labor costs which occurred in this period.

But the change in labor supply conditions had a significance over and beyond the increase in farm labor costs. For, with the migration, the black workers who remained were able to exercise increased occupational selectivity. Thus Seymour Melman in his study of the mechanization process in cotton reported that problems with regard to the supply of labor had affected relations between planters and field hands. He goes on to quote a Delta planter as saying:

The day when a man could protect the grade of his cotton and assume a clean picked crop by threatening his labour with a single-tree or a trace chain has gone forever. The word spreads fast against that kind of planter nowadays and first thing he knows he can't get anybody to pick his cotton.[7]

The significance of such a change in management-labor relations in the plantation South can scarcely be overestimated. The plantation economy rested not merely on coercion, but also upon deference. It was dependency as well as control which characterized the organization of production on the estates. The low wages which prevailed in the region reflected not merely labor abundance and low levels of labor productivity, but the cultural and political subordination of the black population as well. It was this—the debilitating culture of black dependency—which ultimately was uprooted by the black migration from the region. With the heightened bargaining power which that migration vested in the remaining plantation workers, deference became increasingly anachronistic and irrelevant. In turn, labor market relations began for the first time to resemble negotiations between equals, a process which speeded the shedding of the inhibitions which the ideology of dependency had imposed on the black labor force.

The response by the planters to this breakdown in the props underlying the plantation economy was a serious attempt to revolutionize production methods through the adoption of mechanized methods of cultivation and harvesting. With labor increasingly scarce and expensive, with the former docility of their labor force now called into question, the system of incentives facing the producers with regard to the choice of production methods had been irreversibly altered. In effect, the migration north, and the consequent rising cost and increased scarcity of labor, acted as a focusing device. The customary labor-intensive production process was now disrupted, and planters turned their attention to means by which this disruption could be overcome. Now instead of choosing labor-intensive production methods, planters found that investments in tools and machines as complements to the workers was increasingly desirable.

Specifically, the focus of attention was directed to the harvest. This was a process which as late as the 1940s was performed by hand labor and which used about half of the total man-hours needed to produce an acre of cotton. As early as the 1930s a technically proficient harvester had been developed, but was not adopted because of "the absence of cost incentives driving the planters to make the substitution." [8] During World War II such a shift in production methods, though perhaps now desired by the planters, was not feasible because of a shortage of material. But with the end of the war, the demand for a mechanized harvester was quickly identified by potential producers.

International Harvester started making a few harvest machines during the war. According to Street, the fact that this firm was ready to enter into commercial production "coupled with the increasing reports of farm labor shortages heard during the war stimulated a race on the part of other implement firms to get into the market with a similar picker."[9] Deere and Company and Allis Chalmers Manufacturing Company both entered the market with mechanical pickers by the end of the 1940s. The initial price of these machines was between about $6,000 and $7,600, a level which precluded its use for all but the largest and wealthiest cotton planters. By the early 1950s, however, a model appeared at about one-half the initial price and as a result the market for the mechanical picker widened considerably. Table VII.4 reports Street's data on the sale of mechanical picking machines during this period, demonstrating the explosive growth which occurred during these years.[10]

The scope of what mechanization could accomplish in cotton is dramatized in Figure VII.1. Man-hours per bale of cotton under complete mechanization stood at about one-fifth the level that was present when cotton was hand-cultivated and harvested. By

TABLE VII.4   Production of Spindle-type Cotton
Picking Machines in the United States: 1946–1953

Year	Number
1946 and prior years	107
1947	649
1948	766
1949	901
1950	1,527
1951	3,419
1952	4,590
1953	3,741

SOURCE: James H. Street, *The New Revolution in the
Cotton Economy, Mechanization and its Consequences*
(Chapel Hill: The University of North Carolina Press, 1957),
p. 133.

far the most substantial reduction in the required labor input occurred when the cotton boll was mechanically picked, though labor savings were feasible in other stages of cultivation as well.

Aside from mechanization other technological improvements
also were achieved in cotton in the 1940s. These included innovations in the application of fertilizer and improvements in
methods of planting as well as insect control. These improve-

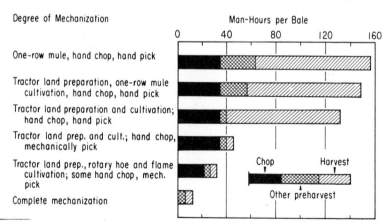

FIGURE VII.1 Reduction of Man Labor through Mechanization (per Bale of
Cotton, Delta Area Mississippi)
SOURCE: U.S. Department of Agriculture, Bureau of Agricultural Economics.

ments in cultivation technique primarily were aimed at increasing yields per acre and it appears that especially in the 1950s these efforts were markedly successful. During that decade output per acre under cotton cultivation increased by slightly more than 60 percent (Table VII.5).

Table VII.5 reveals the sharp break which occurred in labor productivity trends in cotton between 1940 and 1950. As contrasted to the period between 1920 and 1940 when man-hours per acre actually increased, this proxy for mechanization experienced a sharp decline during the 1940s. Disaggregating this measure into preharvest and harvest components again reveals the change in trend which occurred during these years. Between 1920 and 1940 man-hours per acre before the harvest had declined by 16.4 percent. In the ten years between 1940 and 1950 this same measure declined by 28.3 percent. While man-hours per acre in the harvest had actually increased between 1920 and 1940, it declined by 21.2 percent in the 1940s. The upshot of these advances in mechanization was that in the ten years of the 1940s labor productivity in cotton (as measured by man-hours per bale) increased more than in the twenty years between 1920 and 1940, and this occurred despite the fact that advances in yields per acre were slower in the later period than in the earlier.

Richard Day has offered a typology with which to examine the productivity advances that occurred in cotton. This scheme is particularly helpful in accounting for the decline in sharecropping which occurred in this period. Day traces the changes in post-

TABLE VII.5   Man-hours Required in Production of Cotton: 1920–1960

Category	1920	1940	1950	1960
Man-hours per acre	90	98	74	54
Before harvest	55	46	33	23
Harvest	35	52	41	31
Yields of lint per acre (lb.)	160	245	283	454
Man-hours per bale	269	191	126	57

SOURCE: *Historical Statistics of the United States, Colonial Times to 1970*, Part I, Series K93-97 (Washington: Government Printing Office, 1975).

World War II technology through four distinct stages. In stage I, the base point, sharecropping is the organizational basis of production, with the operation mule-powered and the crop hand-picked. In this stage, almost all of the labor required is unskilled. The production process then passes through two intermediate stages. In stage II mechanization of the preharvest processes occurs, particularly on the planter's section of the plantation. In addition, tractor use is introduced in land preparation. The rest of the production process, however, remains traditional with the cultivation remaining largely mule-powered and the harvest still carried out by hand. In stage III complete mechanization of the preharvest operations is introduced, with the hand-picking of the cotton crop the only remaining vestige of long-standing production methods. Finally, the completion of the mechanization process occurs in stage IV. In this stage more than half the manpower required is skilled, representing a fundamental alteration of the labor quality requirements of cultivation.[11]

The transition from one stage to another differed in speed within the region. Nonetheless the process of technological change in cotton in this period was extremely rapid. Day's estimate is that stage IV technology predominated as early as 1955, even though it had been of negligible importance only ten years earlier.[12]

The shift from stage I technology meant the demise of sharecropping. This was so because the shift to stage II and stage III technology radically altered the seasonal distribution of the demand for labor. In stage II mule-powered land preparation and cultivation was eliminated while in stage III the preharvest demand for labor was further reduced. In the meantime, however, in both stages harvest labor demand remained unchanged since no advances occurred in this stage of production. All of this meant that while the demand for labor through most of the crop cycle had been drastically reduced, during the harvest itself the intense need for unskilled labor remained. In turn, according to Day "this meant that the maintenance of sharecroppers the year round became uneconomic."[13] Thus even stage II and stage III technologies, by relieving the pressure of labor demand through much of the crop year, allowed—indeed encouraged—the planters to relax their control over plantation labor and rely instead upon a combination of resident wage labor and hired village labor. This process of relaxation of control was further extended with stage IV technology which resulted in a sharp reduction in the demand for labor over the entire crop cycle. Thus it was that sharecropping came to a rapid demise, the victim of the changing manpower requirements associated with mechanization. As seen in Table VII.6, in the period between 1940 and 1959 the number of black sharecroppers declined by over 225,000—a drop of slightly over 75 percent. By and large, by the early or mid-1960s sharecropping as a form of labor force control had passed into insignificance and so too had the southern plantation economy.

It was during the 1940s then that the technological underpinnings of the plantation economy were dismantled. The revolution in cotton technology which occurred in these years was triggered by the increasing scarcity and cost of plantation labor during the war. Faced with a dramatic change in the relative availability and price of inputs, particularly capital equipment and labor, cotton growers for the first time initiated a large-scale and sustained effort to change methods of production away from their traditional labor-intensive pattern. The result was the mechanization of cotton cultivation and harvest, a process which dramatically reduced the required labor input per unit of cotton production. In turn, this meant the long-standing planter requirement of a large-scale dependent labor force had been ma-

TABLE VII. 6. Southern Sharecroppers by Race: 1930–1959

Category	1930	1940	1945	1950	1954	1959
White cropper	383,381	242,173	176,260	148,708	107,416	47,650
Nonwhite cropper	392,897	299,118	270,296	198,057	160,246	73,387
Total croppers	776,278	541,291	446,556	346,765	267,662	121,037
Percentage nonwhite	50.6	55.3	60.5	57.1	50.9	60.9

SOURCE: *Historical Statistics of the United States, Colonial Times to 1970*, Part I, Series K109–153 (Washington: Government Printing Office, 1975).

terially reduced, thus tending to render anachronistic the institutions and culture of control so long associated with southern agriculture and rural society.

The plantation economy did not collapse at once. The diffusion of the new technology was uneven and took time. Nonetheless the technological requirement for a mass, docile labor force in agriculture had come to an end, thus opening the possibility of the development of a truly new South.

World War II thus represented the beginning of a period of massive social change for the black population in the United States. The black response to the wartime demand for labor had at once triggered the process of labor-displacing technological change in the South and dramatically increased the supply of black labor in the industrial North. Though the escape from and dismantling of the plantation economy potentially symbolized enhanced economic opportunity, these changes obviously were not costless. Especially significant was the fact that the potential which the movement north represented was not accompanied by the kind of public policy and planning necessary to ensure continued economic integration. The future of blacks in the capitalist North was left largely to the whim of the market, a situation which proved to be particularly unfortunate for most of the participants in this wave of labor migration to the industrial economy.

With World War II the log jam had been broken. After decades in which black labor had been constrained to plantation agriculture because of the combined pressures of racist hiring practices, international migration and depression, now finally in the 1940s black labor was urgently needed elsewhere than in the South. This demand overwhelmed the mechanisms of control present in the South and the migration which resulted soon left the southern planters with a scarcity of labor. It was during this wartime period, then, that the southern plantation economy came to an end. Black labor fled the South in search of alternative employment opportunities, which for the first time were available to them. The ensuing migration at once signaled the demise of the control mechanisms of the plantation structure and triggered the onset of the long-delayed mechanization of cotton. The thesis presented here is that the migration was a two-step process. The first step, the movement of black labor in response to wartime demand, doomed the plantation economy. This wartime "pull" triggered the technological changes which resulted in the development of an outward "push" from what formerly was the plantation South.

VIII. POST-PLANTATION BLACK EXPERIENCE

The post-bellum plantation economy was viable in part because the South was able to impose stringent measures of control on the southern black labor force. In addition, the plantation economy rested on the disinterest which northern firms manifested towards the potential availability of southern black labor. The disinclination to recruit and hire black labor came to a halt during World War I and with the closing off of international migration to the United States. As a result, the decades of the 1910s and 1920s saw a substantial outflow of southern blacks from the plantation region. Once again during the 1930s, changes in northern labor market conditions were decisive for what occurred in the South. This time the life of the plantation economy was extended because of the Depression and the resulting decline in the demand for labor. The outflow of black plantation labor was slowed and thus plantation methods of production were able to remain in place. The ultimate breakdown in the plantation structure occurred during World War II when the northern industrial demand for workers produced a massive outflow of black laborers and compelled a major change in production.

The black experience in the United States, then, has never been dissociated from the North. Both the persistence of the plantation economy and the timing of its breakdown were closely related to changes in the northern economy. Given the centrality of the plantation experience in the economic history of blacks in the United States, it follows that blacks too have never been unaffected by the pattern of change which occurred in the North especially as those changes related to the demand for labor.

Before World War II the northern economy affected blacks indirectly via its influence on the plantation economy. After the war, the influence was direct. For with the migration from the South a fundamental change occurred with respect to the occupations filled by black workers. Whereas always in the past the single largest concentration of black labor had lived in the rural South and worked on plantations, now after the war the importance of black agricultural labor declined significantly. By the 1960s most blacks lived in urban areas, a large fraction of whom were in the North and almost all of whom were nonagricultural workers. If, in short, black poverty before World War II was a direct result of participation in the plantation economy, after 1945 that participation represented only a historical legacy to be overcome.

Census estimates are that during the 1950s black migration from the South totalled about 1.5 million in both the 1950s and 1960s, only slightly below the rate of the 1940s.[1] Especially affected by these population movements were the plantation counties. In 1940 immediately preceding the onset of the "push" and "pull" mechanisms, the black population of these counties totalled slightly in excess of 4,000,000, representing 45.3 percent of their total population. By 1970 this number had declined by 12.3 percent to only 3.5 million. In the meantime the white population in these counties had grown rapidly, especially in the newly developing urban centers. Thus by 1970 the proportion of blacks in the plantation counties had declined to only 32.3 percent.[2]

There were two ways in which the legacy of the plantation economy acted to perpetuate black poverty even after the migration from the plantation South. The first is centered on the fact that the long participation by blacks in the plantation structure disproportionately deprived them of ownership of income-earning property. The second is focused on their late arrival in competing for well-paid employment. As late migrants, southern blacks took the last place in line for desirable employment opportunities. Therefore, compared to whites, blacks found themselves with "secondary" labor market jobs, jobs whose defining characteristic often was that the pay was so low that they were shunned by white workers. In combination, these two factors, both ultimately traceable to the longevity of the plantation economy, tended to slow the income gains made by blacks even after their escape from the rural South.

The long historical experience as dependent laborers meant that the migration north was a movement of people most of whom were essentially without property. The income potential of most of the migrants depended upon their ability to sell themselves in the labor market and to collect supplementary benefits from the government. But what they did not possess was the source of substantial income under capitalism: ownership of assets for which they would be paid interest, dividends, profits, or royalties.

As late as 1971 the profound differences by race in the ownership of productive property were manifest.[3] In that year blacks received $53.3 billion, or 6.9 percent of the total money income received by the population. However, blacks received only 0.9 percent of the total income paid in the form of dividends, interest, rents and royalties. Similarly blacks received only 2.9 percent of nonfarm self-employed income and just 0.6 percent of farm self-employed income. When all such forms of property income are combined, the total received by blacks comes to $1.9 billion or about 3.6 percent of total black income from all sources. By contrast property income defined in this way came to 12.7 percent for whites. Thus property income proportionately was 3.5 times greater for whites than blacks.

Even within this category of property income, important differences by race show up. Of all the property income received by whites, 34.3 percent was in the form of dividends, interest, rent, and royalties with the remainder coming from self-employed categories. Only 15.8 percent, by contrast of black property income came from interest, dividends, rent, and royalties. What this means is that not only did blacks receive proportionately less property income, but of that which they did receive, much more than was the case for whites resulted from their owning their own businesses. Whites tended much more to receive their income from sources which required no labor at all.

Economic gains for blacks, then, were dependent upon their ability to move up the occupational hierarchy and secure employment opportunities with relatively high wages or salaries. Table VIII.1 provides some insight into the concentration of blacks in low-income occupations at the time of their massive first entry in-

TABLE VIII.1   Occupational Distribution of the Labor Force by Sex and
Race: 1950

	Male		Female	
Occupation	Black	White	Black	White
Professional, technical and kindred	2.2	7.9	6.2	13.4
Managers, officials and proprietors	2.0	11.6	0.5	4.8
Clerical	3.4	6.8	4.0	29.8
Sales	1.5	6.6	1.3	8.9
Craftsmen, foremen and kindred	7.6	19.3	1.0	1.7
Operatives	20.8	20.0	14.6	19.8
Service except private household	12.5	4.9	17.8	11.4
Laborers	23.1	6.6	1.1	0.7
Private household	0.8	0.1	42.0	4.4
Farm-related	24.8	14.9	10.8	3.0
Not stated	1.3	1.2	0.7	2.2

SOURCE: 1950 Census of the Population.

to the industrial economy. In 1950 less than 5.0 percent of black
male workers were professionals or managers. In contrast, slightly
less than one-fifth of the white male workers were in these
categories. The largest concentration of blacks occurred in the
unskilled and semiskilled categories. Indeed the unskilled categories exceeded the traditional and almost entirely southern farm-
related categories. The semiskilled service work and unskilled
occupations included 56 percent of the 1950 black workers. Among
white workers these same relatively low-paying occupations
accounted for only 31.5 percent of employment.

A similar discrepancy in the occupational structure of the white
and black labor forces occurs among females. Again, as revealed
in the table, there is a conspicuous absence of blacks in the
relatively high-income categories. Yet the most astonishing sta-
tistic is the one for private household work. Slightly more than

two out of every five female workers were found in private house-hold labor—by far the largest concentration. The proportion of black females in this category was almost ten times greater than the proportion of whites in the same occupation.

For both sexes, then, it is clear that the 1950 demand for black labor primarily was to staff low wage occupations. Once so em-ployed, however, the operation of the labor market should, ac-cording to economic theory, permit blacks a comparable upward mobility to that experienced by whites. However, the ability of these new recruits to be fully integrated into the host society depends upon two crucial variables. The first is whether a future cycle of rapid economic growth is experienced, thus allowing the immigrant group to replicate the occupational mobility of the original labor force. The second is the extent to which the hos-tility generated against the immigrant group produces obstacles to their taking advantage of the potential provided by rapid growth rates.

Data on the occupational distribution of the labor force for 1970 shown in Table VIII.2 indicate the extent to which blacks were able to move up the occupational hierarchy in the years be-tween 1950 and 1970. A substantial degree of upward mobility is obvious. For black males the percentage share in the four top occupations more than doubled and the ratio of the percentage of whites to blacks in these categories fell from 3.5 to 2.0. Similarly for females there was a vast movement out of the low-status pri-vate household category and a comparably large movement into the clerical category. At the same time, however, especially for black men the concentration in relatively poorly paid occupations except for agriculture continued to prevail. In both 1950 and 1970 about two-thirds of the working black males were found in such jobs. Indeed the ratio of the percentage of blacks compared to whites in these categories actually increased from 1.59 in 1950 to 1.72 in 1970.

The 1970 data suggest that blacks are no longer exclusively confined to the low-level jobs which were available to them upon their initial movement north. At the same time the continuing concentration of blacks at relatively low occupational levels also suggests that nothing like a full process of occupational integration has occurred. Furthermore, a detailed study of the occupations into which blacks have moved reveals that "in most categories the greatest gains were made in the least prestigious and least paid occupations."[4] On the basis of the trend between 1950 and 1970, therefore, it appears unlikely that the relative under-representation of blacks at high level jobs will soon be eliminated, even though there have been some breakthroughs. Nor does it seem obvious that the over-representation of blacks at the low end of the distribution will be eliminated in the near future. The result is that while there is a widening of the range of occupations realistically within the grasp of individual black workers, black laborers as a group continue to fill the role of providing relatively low level labor within the economic system. The degree to which there has been a movement of blacks to high level jobs may be viewed as the result of the relatively rapid rates of economic growth experienced in the United States especially in the 1960s.

TABLE VIII.2   Occupational Distribution of the Labor Force by Sex and Race: 1970

	Male		Female	
Occupation	Black	White	Black	White
Professional, technical and kindred	7.8	14.6	10.8	15.0
Managers, officials and proprietors	4.7	14.3	1.9	4.8
Clerical	7.4	7.1	20.8	36.4
Sales	1.8	6.1	2.5	7.7
Craftsmen, foremen and kindred	13.8	20.8	0.8	1.2
Operatives	28.3	18.7	17.6	14.1
Service except private household	12.8	6.0	25.6	15.3
Laborers	17.5	6.2	0.7	0.4
Private household	0.1	0.3	17.5	3.4
Farm-related	5.3	5.6	0.8	0.7
Not stated	0.5	0.3	1.0	1.0

SOURCE: Bureau of Labor Statistics, *Handbook of Labor Statistics*, 1971.

At the same time, the continued role played by blacks as the providers of relatively low paid work stands as a continuing testimony to the legacy of the plantation economy, and the failure of the capitalist economy adequately to absorb this new black labor force.

IX. STRATEGIES OF CHANGE

This study has concentrated on analyzing the structural determinants of black poverty. The hypothesis has been that the southern black population was victimized by the structure of southern society. The plantation economy that prevailed after the Civil War was similar, but not identical, to the slave system that prevailed before 1861. Though domination in this way was real, and southern blacks were the victims of southern history, an analysis of that victimization does not tell the whole story. There was a response by the black population to oppression, as for example, in the case of the organization of the sharecroppers' union discussed above. Thus a complete assessment of the roots of black poverty requires a consideration of the attempts by the black population to overcome that poverty.

The strategies which are appropriate for the alleviating of poverty depend upon the causes of that deprivation. This study has suggested that although poverty has been the fate of most black people in the United States since the Civil War, its causes have varied over time. In the years between the Civil War and World War II poverty was the consequence of entrapment in the plantation economy. After 1940 poverty persisted, but now was the result of the skewed absorption of black labor into the capitalist North's occupational structure. Thus the strategies which suggested themselves to the black population as appropriate for reducing poverty in the first period were different from those which were available after the breakdown of the plantation economy.

In the aftermath of the Civil War two major alternatives suggested themselves to southern blacks as a means to escape poverty. The first was migration, an escape from the low-paying occupations of the plantations to more remunerative jobs elsewhere. The second was a search for pockets of potential prosperity

within the southern economy. Spokesmen for the second viewpoint argued that by preparing themselves morally and edu-
cationally for these opportunities southern blacks would be able
to advance economically. What limited both of these approaches
was that they assumed stability in the plantation economy. The
first, in despairing of change to that structure, saw advance
possible only through escape; the other hoped that, by exploring
the opportunities that were available within the plantation system,
black gains could be attained.

Land ownership was the universally acknowledged goal of the
ex-slave population. Vernon Wharton has written of the ex-slaves
that "their very lives were entwined with the land and its cultivation; they lived in a society where respectability was based on
ownership of the soil; and to them to be free was to farm their own
ground."[1] Not only did the desire for land represent a means to
attain social status, it also represented the most obvious strategy
for escaping poverty, for if land had been distributed to the former slaves, that population would have been permitted to participate as entrepreneurs in the nineteenth century market for
cotton. The extent of the prosperity which would then have
accrued to the black population would have depended on such
factors as the strength of the market, the entrepreneurial capabil-
ities of the freedmen, and the quality of the soil under cultivation.
It seems reasonable to assume in such circumstances that the
virtually uniform poverty that affected black sharecroppers after
the Civil War would not have existed under a regime of extensive
black land ownership. In all likelihood the opportunity to generate
and share in property income in cotton would have resulted in
significant income differentials emerging within the black population representing the range of successful and unsuccessful
commercial farmers.

That a program of land redistribution to the ex-slave population was not adopted meant two things. The first was that black
agricultural workers were to continue to be made available to the
estates under adverse conditions. This enabled the structure of
the plantation economy to remain intact; as a result, low incomes
prevailed. Second, for the black population, as under slavery, the

perpetuation of the plantation system enforced a common economic experience on many black workers, an experience separate and distinct from that of most white workers in the rest of the country. Confinement to the southern plantation system thus meant that occupational integration was prevented, continuing the racial division which has characterized the American working class since slavery.

Despite the fact that the absence of a radical reform of the structure of land ownership in the South prevented black commercial farmers from developing in large numbers, the goal of land ownership was integral to black economic strategies in the nineteenth century. For it was hoped that through the ownership of land, successful black businessmen could be brought into existence. Thus, August Meier in his discussion of black thought in this period cites a statement issued by a national convention of black leaders, meeting in 1897, as representative: "We are to a great extent the architects of our own fortunes, and must rely mainly upon our own exertions for success." The statement went on to recommend that "the youth of our race [adopt] a strict morality, temperate habits and the practice of the acquisition of land . . . and advancing to mercantile positions and forcing their way into various productive channels of literature, art, science, and mechanics."[2]

Racial solidarity was an integral part of this approach. Since there were relatively few business opportunities for blacks in the South, it was important under this strategy that black consumers patronize black businesses. One black lawyer at the same convention cited by Meier put it this way: "We must help one another. Our industries must be patronized and our laborers encouraged. . . . We are laboring for race elevation and race unity is the all important factor."[3] Thus the strategy of finding entrepreneurial opportunities within the plantation structure for a few businessmen depended upon the entire group's support for such aspiring individuals.

The ultimate expression of the concept of self-help and individual advance during this period came from Booker T. Washington. Washington believed that southern blacks should deliber-

ately refrain from political participation and, at least in the short
run, accommodate themselves to the southern social structure.
Instead of attempting to change the South, he believed that they
should learn skills and enter trades in order to compete economically. In his view it was only after having reacquired skills
possessed during slavery but presumably lost in the post-bellum
period, that blacks would be equipped to attain and use their
constitutional rights. As a result, Washington was a leading
proponent of establishing industrial schools for blacks and was at
the forefront of a movement to endow such schools with philan-
thropic funding. According to Meier, Washington, despite his
acceptance of white political domination, did not think in terms
of a subordinate place in the American economy for blacks; rather,
"he thought in terms of developing a substantial propertied class
of landowners and businessmen."[4]

The need for self-help and group solidarity was, of course,
imposed upon the black population by the plantation organization
of the South. At the same time this strategy reflected the continued ideological hegemony of paternalism. Most markedly this
was the case with Washington. For despite Meier's claim to the
contrary, at least in his immediate circumstances and especially
in the political sphere, Washington did accept a subordinate role
for the black population. His outlook was thoroughly southern
and agricultural, searching for opportunities within the existing
structure. Within the limits imposed by his accepting the plantation hegemony as a permanent system, Washington's response
was a creative one. But in failing to break out of those limits, even
in his imagination, Washington was unable to offer an approach
which could transcend systemically imposed mass poverty.

Self-help and the creation of a class of black businessmen
represent at least a potential means for some blacks to overcome
plantation-induced poverty. Even aside from the limited numbers who could benefit, however, there was a major weakness in
this approach. The success of self-help ultimately depended not
only on the blacks' successfully endowing themselves with skills,
but also on the creation of opportunities for the skills to be put to
profitable use. But there was nothing in the strategy that spoke to

this problem, for ultimately the limited opportunities available to blacks in the South were a function of the plantation structure. Changes in that structure implied the use of political means—a route which Washington deliberately ruled out. Equipping blacks with the skills which would allow them to be successful commercial farmers, for example, did not mean that any more good land would be made available to them. There was, in short, an assumption which underlay the self-help strategy that was almost certainly unwarranted. It was that, once blacks were properly socialized and endowed with appropriate skills, the structure of the southern economy was sufficiently flexible to accommodate upwardly mobile individuals. Obviously this may have been the case for a few. But our analysis of the plantation economy suggests that the assumption was probably incorrect if the hope was that through such means the widespread poverty among southern blacks was to be alleviated.

It was W. E. B. DuBois who saw that accommodation to the plantation structure was inconsistent with economic advance. It was therefore DuBois who, in advocating struggle for blacks to achieve equality in all spheres of life, became the spokesman for those who wanted to break with the culture of the plantation economy.

The ballot, DuBois argued, was the least "a guilty nation could grant a wronged race" and the only method of compelling the South to accept the results of the Civil War.[5] DuBois attacked the individual planks of Washington's program. He argued that it was "utterly impossible" to create a class of black businessmen and property holders who could defend their gains without the right of suffrage. Similarly Washington's desire for thrift and self-respect, argued DuBois, was at variance to his counsel of "silent submission to civil inferiority" since such self-denial was "bound to sap the manhood of any race in the long-run."[6] Finally, DuBois noted that the common and industrial schools advocated by Washinton were dependent upon the existence of Negro colleges for teachers.[7] Thus DuBois argued in opposition to Washington with regard to the vote, civic equality and education, and asserted that failure to participate in the struggle for political rights undermined the chances of attaining Washington's own goals. But the fact that DuBois advocated struggle and Washington accomodation is evidence of the contrasting world views held by each: Washington's, that of the plantation economy; and Dubois', that of a wider society in which blacks fought to attain their legitimate aspirations.

The emphasis on uplift and on the development of a class of black businessmen characteristic of Washington's thought has been interpreted as a kind of black nationalism.[8] Indeed, on at least one occasion Washington himself asserted, "We are a nation within a nation," and like other advocates of self-help encouraged black patronage of black business establishments.[9] Yet it is important not to confuse a concern for the emergence of black businesses and farms with the advocacy of political separation and self-government, normally the salient characteristics of nationalist movements. For self-help represents a response to imposed separation and stands as a strategy to achieve advances within that structure. Nationalism, on the contrary, sees separation and self-rule as its goals. These ends were explicitly rejected by Washington.

Thus, it is hard to describe nineteenth and early twentieth century self-help advocates, especially Washington, as nationalists. This undoubtedly was a period of turning inward by strategists of black advance. But the racial solidarity which was thus manifest was only a means to attain the ultimate end of advance within southern society and was not intended to be the base upon which a self-governing black nation was to be constructed.

Self-help was a southern strategy, one which accepted the structure of the plantation economy. Advocates of migration from the South also accepted the permanence of the plantation economy as did Washington, but unlike the latter did not believe that the black population should remain in that structure. In a sense, of course, migration also is a form of self-help. Yet the underlying assumption of migration is pessimism with regard to the opportunities for success in the South, precisely contrary to Washington's views on the subject. The advocacy of migration to the North in order to take industrial employment opportunities represented therefore an alternative to self-help in the search for economic advance.

As we have seen, the steady flow of European immigrants to the United States, in combination with the constraints imposed on blacks in the South, had effectively foreclosed migration as a viable strategy before World War I. With the coming of the war, this imposed immobility was relaxed. The increase in the demand for black labor which occurred with the curtailing of immigration during the war provided the first test of migration as a means for overcoming southern rural poverty. The excitement and anticipation which the opportunity to migrate generated among southern blacks indicate that for many this approach was seen as a more realistic opportunity than was suggested by Washington's self-help program.

The single most important spokesman who called for the northward flow of black labor was Robert Abbott. Abbott was editor and publisher of the *Chicago Defender*, the most widely read and influential black newspaper during this period. Through the pages of the *Defender*, Abbott urged blacks to "come North where there is more humanity, some justice and fairness."[10] Through the newspaper he organized the Great Northern Drive—a campaign to induce such a migration. Through such efforts as well as prominent coverage of black victimization in the South, Abbott advocated migration. The *Defender*, according to Florette Henri, "in news items, anecdotes, cartoons and photos . . . crystallized the underlying economic and social causes of black suffering into immediate motives for flight."[11] The *Defender*, for example, frequently published poems in support of the cause such as the anonymously written fifteen-stanza "Bound for the Promised Land," one stanza of which is reproduced below.

> Why should I remain longer south
> To be kicked and dogged around?
> Crackers to knock me in the mouth
> And shoot my brother down.
> I would rather the cold to snatch my breath
> And die from natural cause
> Than to stay down south and to be beat to death
> Under cracker laws.[12]

By World War I and its aftermath, then, three basic strategies of change had been articulated: self-help, political struggle, and migration. By this time some evidence had already accumulated that large numbers of American blacks would choose if they were able, some form of migration as the means by which they would try to escape poverty. Self-help and the establishing of black businesses in the South seemed unlikely to touch most blacks' lives in a significant manner. At the same time the continued dominance of the plantation way of life in the South meant that chances for success in political struggle seemed remote. But the black migratory response to the changed labor market circumstances associated with the curtailing of immigration did represent an effective response to distinctly bleak circumstances. It was a response which at once reflected a search for improved living conditions but which entertained little hope for finding or achieving such improvement in the South.

The upsurge of migration which occurred during World War I indicated that large numbers of blacks were not willing to accept Washington's advice that they remain in the South. Yet the ghettoized and deprived conditions which awaited blacks in the North meant that their sense of group identity did not dissipate. The same group deprivation which Washington had seized upon in formulating his self-help strategy for the South persisted in the North as racism in employment, education, and housing manifested itself in the industrial centers to which the blacks moved. Thus by the 1920s many blacks had shown themselves to be mobile while still continuing to possess a sense of group solidarity.

It was both group solidarity and willingness to migrate which underlay yet another strategy offered to the black population, that associated with the name of Marcus Garvey. Garvey's politics evolved over a period of time, but a full statement of his mature views appeared in 1923. He rejected the approach which "sought to teach the Negro to aspire to social equality with whites," arguing that "this has been the source of much trouble." He went on: "The time is opportune to regulate the relationship between both races. Let the Negro have a country of his own. Help him to return to his original home, Africa, and there give him the opportunity to climb from the lowest to the highest positions in a state of his own."[13] Thus the position neatly combined the sense of group solidarity already noticed by Washington and self-help strategists with the observation that American blacks were willing to migrate to search out an improved standard of living. Now, however, in Garvey's formulation, self-help had become nationhood while migration had become a return to the blacks' "orginal home," Africa.

By about 1920 Garvey's United Negro Improvement Association with its combined advocacy of group solidarity and migration to Africa had become the most important black organization in the country. The fact that the organization failed to find an outlet for American blacks in Africa is not of immediate relevance here. More significant is the means by which Garvey's movement succeeded in mobilizing large numbers of blacks. As Harold Cruse puts it,

. . . adopting what he wanted from Washington's ideas, Garvey carried them further—advocating Negro self-sufficiency in the United States linked this time, with the idea of regaining access to the African homeland, as a basis for constructing a viable black economy.[14]

As he did with regard to Washington, DuBois too stood in opposition to the Garveyite movement. The main issue in this case was the nature of the African homeland, an especially important argument since DuBois also was a Pan-Africanist, though in a very different manner than Garvey. Garvey's biographer Elton C. Fax has described their differences very well.

Both DuBois and Garvey were Pan-Africanists. The difference separating them was this: DuBois' Pan-Africanism was designed as an aid to African national self-determination under African leadership for the benefit of Africans themselves. Garvey's Pan-Africanism envisioned the movement as one in which Africa would be the place where black peoples of the Western world would colonize and where Garvey and his U. N. I. A. would head the program of Colonization, with the consent and cooperation of African leaders.[15]

In addition to their contrasting views with regard to Africa, DuBois and Garvey sharply disagreed—in a manner reminiscent of the DuBois-Washington disagreement—over the utility of political struggle in the United States. Garvey noted DuBois' belief in the efficacy of action to achieve social and political equality. Garvey believed, however, that such struggle was doomed to failure since "reason dictates that the masses of the white race will never stand by the ascendency of an opposite minority group to favored positions in a government, society and industry that exists by the will of the majority." He went on to say that "the demand of the DuBois group of colored leaders will only lead ultimately to further disturbances in riots, lynchings and mob rule."[16] From this it followed that political involvement was fruitless. Garvey therefore argued that the only logical solution to the plight of the black population was emigration.

The Garveyite movement was relatively short-lived. For a variety of reasons that need not detain us here, it had shrunk in size considerably by the time Garvey himself was deported from the United States in 1927. Despite its rapid demise, however, the Garveyite ideology represented a major new departure in black thinking. With Garvey the sense of self and community, which had previously supported the self-help concept, now received a more complete expression as nationhood. The black experience was sufficiently similar over the entire black population, reasoned Garvey, that it cemented individuals together culturally as well as economically. From this was derived a belief that members of this group could not only join together to help one another, for example, as consumers, but could also forge a common nation. In the Garvey formulation the locus of this nation was Africa, but location was not as important as the fact that Garvey had fully articulated a nationalist position. What was crucial was the full expression of the latent nationalism which was present in self-help, but which had not before been fully articulated because its spokesmen such as Washington had accepted a subordinate role in southern society.

Finally, it was the United States Communist Party which provided a program of political struggle which was attractive to many southern blacks. In a sense, therefore, this party crystallized DuBois' attitude toward political action. Robert L. Allen notes that during the late 1920s and early 1930s, "the Communist Party succeeded in establishing itself for a time as the leading advocate of equal rights for black people." According to Allen it did so on the basis of a position which it adopted in 1928 in which the party supported a program of Black Belt self-determination.[17] A resolution passed by the Party in that year said that:

> . . . while continuing and intensifying the struggle under the slogan of full social and political equality for the Negroes . . . the Party must come out openly and unreservedly for the right of Negroes to self-determination in the Southern states where the Negroes form a majority of the population. . . .[18]

In this connection James Allen published a study which identified the Black Belt as the locus of the incipient black nation. In the process he pointed to the special circumstances in which black agricultural workers found themselves in this region. In effect, through James Allen's study, the Communist Party identified what we have called the plantation economy as the cause of black poverty. At the same time it argued that it was precisely in the deep South that the black population by seizing the instruments of government could fashion means to alleviate its poverty.[19]

This, of course, was the ultimate break with paternalism and dependency; for this position affirmed that the black population was southern and need not migrate in order to achieve its rights. It argued that blacks through struggle could make the South their own and recreate it as they chose. It was a position which resembled that of DuBois, though it made the nationalist content of the position more explicit than DuBois typically did. The program thus was a most radical departure from paternalism since it argued that power in the South need not remain with the former masters but could be seized by the black population itself.

There is a question with regard to how significant the nationalist position was in the Party's day-to-day activities. For example, Robert Allen has written that "the Communists . . . did not press the program of self-determination of the Black Belt and instead concentrated on trade union and antidiscrimination struggles."[20] But this issue need not detain us here. The fact is that the Communist Party did articulate a southern strategy that broke with paternalism, and apparently the Party's approach influenced significant numbers of southern blacks.

The Communist Party ultimately withdrew its Black self-determination position in 1958. By that time, however, self-determination had been rendered moot. Strategies for black advance were required now to confront the new circumstances facing the black population: geographic dispersion and the end of the southern plantation economy. In the meantime, however, through the spokesmen we have discussed, as well as many others, the black population in the South had been offered important alternative ways to think about itself other than as permanent semi-slaves in a plantation economy.

X. CURRENT PROSPECTS

With the huge migratory movement which occurred during and after World War II the locus of the black problem had changed. While significant numbers remained in the South, a rapidly increasing percentage of blacks had come to reside in the industrial centers of the North and West. At once this migration represented an attempt to enhance standards of living and had profound implications for the development of future strategies of advance. As we have seen, the movement of the black population out of the South deeply affected the social structure of that region—doing no less than ending the southern plantation economy. At the same time it resulted in the settling of masses of black people in a new, for them, mode of production. Thus for those who remained in the South social relations had changed, while for those who moved North new conditions of deprivation were encountered.

It was in this dynamic context that the civil rights movement emerged. What is most salient about that movement, in retrospect, is the fact that it was predominantly a southern movement. For example, Mary Ellison notes that when "non-violent demonstrations against all forms of discrimination flowered in the South during the early sixties . . . always prominent among the leaders of passive resistance was Martin Luther King who donated a philosophy and a certain easy eloquent style that gave voice to the mood of Southern blacks."[1] Thus the most important and sustained political effort by the black population in the post-World War II period was essentially regionally specific. It represented a sustained, and often heroic effort, to achieve equality under the law in a region where legal inequality under the law had long provided the undergirding for the society.

The South of the 1950s and 1960s was not the South of a former epoch. The migratory movement which had started in the 1910s and swelled in the post-World War II period had set in motion forces fundamentally changing the structure of southern society.

For the region as a whole the demise of the plantation economy allowed for the initiation of a dynamic process of economic growth. As a result the demand for relatively high productivity labor increased, making the former mechanisms of labor control increasingly anachronistic. At the same time the breakdown of the plantation economy meant enhanced opportunity for industrial and occupational mobility for blacks. The same forces that increased the demand for industrial labor created conditions in which blacks found it easier to supply themselves for such employment opportunities.

It seems likely that the emergence of the civil rights movement had its roots in the breakdown of the plantation economy. With that collapse the structural underpinnings of deference and paternalism were once and for all destroyed. As a result the behavior the plantation economy called for was exposed as unnecessary and even humiliating. The operative mechanisms by which this change in southern social structure gave rise to the civil rights movement may have been along two paths. First, by facilitating some degree of geographic, educational or economic mobility, the breakdown may have produced an enhanced sense of outrage at the legal constraints which continued to oppress southern blacks. As the southern black population became increasingly mobile and involved in the industrial capitalist economy, the ideology of subservience which was embodied in southern paternalism must have become increasingly unacceptable. The systematic discrimination which continued may have come to be seen as intolerable precisely as mobility and increased opportunity became real possibilities for increasing numbers of blacks. Second, the very same process may have divided the white leadership of the southern society, thus making it easier for blacks to make advances. The leaders of southern society apparently divided into two groups: those defending traditional southern constraints and those who identified with the needs of the emerging industrial capitalism of the region. Those in the latter group tended to accept the breakdown of the old way of life in the interest of the more efficient social organization characteristic of market-dominated capitalism.

It was, however, because the civil rights movement was essentially addressing the vestiges of the plantation economy that it was relatively unsuccessful in addressing the issues of poverty and deprivation experienced by blacks in the industrial North and West. Issues such as the vote and access to public accommodations spoke to the mechanisms of social control integral to the plantation economy, but typically not essential to the functioning of the more advanced capitalist North. Seen in this way, it is at once apparent how the civil rights movement was able to build the extensive coalition which was present, for example, at the 1963 Washington March, but at the same time failed to have much of an impact on the lives of the already ghettoized northern blacks. Racial discrimination in the South provided a target against which a wide spectrum of northern support could be generated. But because the archaic institutions of the plantation economy were not operative elsewhere, and indeed were of decreasing relevance in the rapidly growing South of the 1960s, the impact of this movement was confined, and the problems of northern poverty and exploitation generally were not effectively raised. The unstructured riots which swept the northern urban areas during the 1960s served as testimony to the humiliating degradation which existed outside of the South. But at the same time these same events tended to point to the relative impotence of the civil rights movement in addressing the problems of the northern black population.

The causes of black poverty in the North were fundamentally different from those in the South. The historic reasons for black poverty had been entrapment as agricultural laborers in the southern plantation structure. This meant that the development of the region's productive forces was constrained, confining most of its population and especially the black population to low levels of income. In the North, on the contrary, the perpetuation of poverty among blacks could not be assigned to an insufficient degree of economic development. Rather, as we have seen, the problem lay in the fact that blacks, as they migrated, owned relatively little productive property, while their absorption into the occupational structure of the North was skewed in the direction of low-paying jobs. The problems of the blacks in the North were not related to anachronistic restrictions impeding the development of the whole economy, but rather to the positions they occupied in the labor force.

One obvious source of this skewed absorption into the labor force was racial discrimination. There is now abundant statistical evidence to demonstrate that such discrimination is significant in accounting for the maldistribution of black labor. Some economists have gone further than the mere citation of such data and have argued that discrimination is endemic to the capitalist system. In developing this argument they point to the advantages such discrimination provides to management in its relations with labor. By driving a racial cleavage into the ranks of workers, the development of class solidarity is inhibited and managerial prerogatives thus kept intact. Yet at least on theoretical grounds questions can be raised with respect to the essentiality of racial discrimination under capitalism. The very process of segmenting the labor market, while producing vertical fissures among the working class, tends also to produce conditions of labor scarcity for at least some job categories. Those occupations to which blacks do not have access will depend entirely upon white sources of supply. Where the demand for such work is intense, it is quite conceivable that the exclusion of a numerically significant grouping of workers such as blacks may create a condition of insufficient labor supply. As a result employer discrimination may result in an increase in labor costs which otherwise could be avoided if discrimination were eliminated. Without denying, therefore, that discrimination is present and is an important source of black poverty in the North, it seems unlikely that such behavior is systemic in the sense that it is impossible to eliminate under capitalism.

If we assume for the moment that all forms of employer discrimination were to disappear, the question still remains whether poverty can be eliminated among blacks under capitalism. Two issues appear to be determinant in this regard. The first is the set of circumstances which affect the supply of labor—in particular, the ability of the black population to receive the training and education which would make them valuable resources to prospective employers. The second is the question of the future expansion in the demand for labor. Lying behind this is the rate of expansion of the economy as a whole. For in the future, as in the past, economic gains among blacks depend upon their unemployment rate being low, a condition which exists only when the rate of economic expansion is high and labor markets are tight.[2] Thus if it were possible to believe that in the future educational facilities available to blacks would be upgraded to the point that they could compete as equals with whites in the labor market and that the demand for labor would be sufficiently buoyant so that full employment were to prevail, it would be possible to project a period of continued economic advance for blacks.

To state these conditions, however, is to produce disquiet with regard to the prospects for future black economic advance. For the two keys to continued economic advance confront precisely the basic problematic of the contemporary American capitalist economy: its capacity to maintain low rates of unemployment, while at the same time finding the resources to provide an adequately funded public sector. In our case the latter refers specifically to the resources necessary to modernize the deteriorating educational facilities in major urban settings. This obviously is not the place to explore these issues in depth. But if the future produces a continued high rate of unemployment and an insufficient improvement in public education, then such trends cannot help but impair future black economic advance.

The dynamic of change in the American society has placed the black working class in a difficult half-way position. Only one generation or so removed from the plantation economy, nothing like full occupational integration has occurred and the black working class remains disproportionately in low-wage jobs. At the same time opportunities for advancement undoubtedly are superior in the context of industrial capitalism than they were in the rural South. The number of individuals moving upward occupationally, though relatively small, is not unimportant and may be large enough to feed and make credible similar aspirations among wide numbers of potential black workers. A shutting off of such avenues of advance may produce a political reaction among these aspiring individuals if they find themselves increasingly frustrated.

The political consequences of a high unemployment rate and

inadequate public education are, of course, difficult to predict. One thing is clear, however; such trends, though disproportionately affecting the black population, could not be experienced by that segment of the American population alone. White workers, too, depend upon economic growth to secure the employment opportunities essential for their well-being. Similarly the overwhelming majority of white households depend upon public education to secure the skills that allow them to be effective labor market participants. Continued high levels of unemployment and an insufficient commitment to public education would cause deprivation among workers of all races.

If, in short, the black prospect for economic advance declines—contingent as such prospects are on steady economic growth—that decline will have major repercussions for the nonblack population as well. In turn, such developments may give rise to a politics in which the historical black/white racial division is overcome in the light of the common interests shared by both groups. Conditions giving rise to the failure of the black population to secure economic gains may provide the basis upon which a biracial political movement in search of jobs and income may be constructed in the United States.

Much stands in the way of such a development. Racism is deeply imbedded in western culture. It is not easy to be confident that a centuries-old set of beliefs and stereotypes will be overcome easily by awareness of increasing occupational convergence and shared economic interests between blacks and whites. Similarly it seems unlikely that the consciousness of the long history of shared exploitation among blacks which has given rise to nationalist politics will be dissipated quickly. Nonetheless the structural position of both groups is increasingly similar. This raises the possibility that such negative historical legacies may be overcome, as each group finds its economic interests to be identical with that of the other for the first time in American history.

APPENDIX

I. Number of Counties by State—578

	Total Counties	Plantation Counties
Alabama	67	47
Arkansas	75	23
Georgia	146	70
Louisiana	60	29
Mississippi	79	45
N. Carolina	98	21
S. Carolina	43	35

total plantation counties 270
total nonplantation counties 298

II. Individual Plantation Counties—by States

ALABAMA

Autauga	Dallas	Marengo
Barbour	Dekalb	Marshall
Bibb	Elmore	Montgomery
Butler	Green	Morgan
Calhoun	Hale	Perry
Chambers	Henry	Pickens
Cherokee	Houston	Pike
Clarke	Jackson	Randolph
Clay	Lauderdale	Russel
Cleburne	Lawrence	Sumter
Coffee	Lee	Talladega
Colbert	Limestone	Tallapoosa
Coosa	Lowndes	Tuscaloosa
Crenshaw P	Macon	Wilcox
Dale	Madison	

ARKANSAS

Arkansas	Jackson	Mississippi
Ashley	Jefferson	Monroe
Chicot	Lafayette	Phillips

Crittenden
Cross
Desha
Drew
Hempstead

Lee
Lincoln
Little River
Lonoke
Miller

Prairie
Pulaski
St. Francis
Woodruff

GEORGIA

Baker
Banks
Bibb
Brooks
Bulloch
Burke
Butts
Calhoun
Chattechouchee
Clarke
Clay
Crawford
Decatur
Dodge
Dooley
Dougherty
Early
Elbert
Emanuel
Franklin
Grady

Greene
Gwinnett
Hall
Hancock
Harris
Hart
Henry
Houston
Jackson
Jasper
Jenkins
Johnson
Lee
Macon
Madison
Marion
Meriwether
Miller
Mitchell
Morgan
Muscogee

Newton
Oconee
Oglethorpe
Pulaski
Putman
Randolph
Rockdale
Schley
Screven
Stewart
Talbot
Taliaferro
Terrell
Thomas
Troup
Twiggs
Walton
Washington
Webster
Wilkes
Worth
Quitman

LOUISIANA

Acadia
Avoyelles
Bossier
Caddo
Catahoula
Concordia
East Baton Rouge
East Carroll
East Felicianna
Iberia

Iberville
Lafayette
Madison
Morehouse
Natchitoches
Ouachita
Pointe Couppe
Rapides
Red River
Richland

St. Helena
St. Landry
St. Martin
St. Mary
Tensas
West Baton Rouge
West Carroll
West Feliciana
Franklin

MISSISSIPPI

Adams	Issaquena	Ponotoc
Amite	Jefferson	Prentiss
Attala	Kemper	Quitman
Bolivar	Lafayette	Rankin
Carroll	Lee	Sharkey
Chickasaw	Leflore	Sunflower
Claiborne	Lincoln	Tallahatchie
Clay	Lowndes	Tate
Couhorna	Madison	Tunica
Copiah	Marshall	Union
Desota	Monroe	Warren
Franklin	Montgomery	Washington
Grenada	Noxubee	Wilkinson
Hinds	Okitbbeita	Yalobusha
Holmes	Panola	Yazoo

NORTH CAROLINA

Anson	Robeson	Harnett
Bladen	Sampson	Johnson
Cumberland	Scotland	Lenoir
Duplin	Union	Mecklenburg
Edgecombe	Wake	Nash
Greene	Wayne	Pitt
Halifax	Wilson	Richmond

SOUTH CAROLINA

Abbeville	Dillon	Newberry
Aiken	Edgefied	Oconee
Allendale	Fairfield	Orangeburg
Anderson	Florence	Pickens
Bamberg	Greenville	Richland
Barnwell	Kershaw	Saluda
Calhoun	Lancaster	Spartansburg
Cherokee	Laurens	Sumter
Chester	Lee	Union
Chesterfield	Lexington	Williamsburg
Clarendon	Marion	York
Darlington	Marlboro	

NOTES

PREFACE

1. Jay R. Mandle, *The Plantation Economy: Population and Economic Change in Guyana, 1838–1960* (Philadelphia: Temple University Press, 1973).
2. George L. Beckford, *Persistent Poverty: Underdevelopment in Plantation Economies of the Third World* (New York: Oxford University Press, 1972).
3. Charles Wagley, "Plantation America: A Culture Sphere," in Vera Rubin, ed., *Caribbean Studies—A Symposium* (Seattle: University of Washington, 1960).

I. THE PLANTATION MODE OF PRODUCTION

1. Maurice Dobb, *Studies in the Development of Capitalism* (New York: International Publishers, 1947), p. 7.
2. Eugene D. Genovese, *The World the Slaveholders Made* (New York: Vintage Books, 1971), p. 18.
3. ———, *In Red and Black: Marxian Explorations in Southern and Afro-American History* (New York: Vintage Books, 1971), p. 324 (emphasis added, J.R.M.)
4. *Ibid.*, p. 406.
5. ———. *Roll, Jordan, Roll: The World the Slaves Made* (New York: Pantheon, 1974), p. 661.
6. Immanuel Wallerstein, *The Modern World-System Capitalist Agriculture and the Origins of the European World-Economy in the Sixteenth Century* (New York: Academic Press, 1974), pp. 126-27.
7. *Ibid.*, p. 350.
8. *Ibid.*, p. 162.
9. Maurice Dobb, "Transition from Feudalism to Capitalism," in Maurice Dobb, ed., *Papers on Capitalism, Development and Planning* (New York: International Publishers, 1967), pp. 2-3.
10. Dobb, *Studies*, p. 7. (See also fn. 1.)
11. William O. Jones, "Plantation," in David Sills, ed., *The International Encyclopedia of the Social Sciences* 12 (1968), pp. 154–55.
12. Edgar T. Thompson, "The Plantation: The Physical Basis of Traditional Race Relations,' in Edgar T. Thompson, ed., *Race Relations and the Race Problem, A Definition and an Analysis* (Durham, N.C.: Duke University Press, 1939), pp. 191–193. (Available from Greenwood Press, New York.)
13. Richard S. Dunn, *Sugar and Slaves: The Rise of the Planter Class in the English West Indies, 1624–1713* (Chapel Hill: The University of North Carolina Press, 1972), pp. 71-74.
14. George L. Beckford, *Persistent Poverty: Underdevelopment in Plantation Economies of the Third World* (New York: Oxford University Press, 1972), p. 34.
15. Thompson, *Race Relations*, pp. 192-94. (See also fn. 12.)
16. For a discussion of this process see Jay R. Mandle, *The Plantation Economy: Population and Economic Change in Guyana, 1838–1960* (Philadelphia: Temple University Press, 1973).

II. OBSTACLES TO BLACK MIGRATION

1. Lawanda Cox and John A. Cox, *Politics, Principle and Prejudice: 1865–66* (New York: Free Press of Glencoe, Macmillan, 1963).

2. Oscar Zeichner, "The Transition from Slave to Free Agricultural Labor in the Southern States," *Agricultural History*, 13:26 (January 1939).

3. George Bentley, *A History of the Freedmen's Bureau* (Philadelphia: University of Pennsylvania Press, 1955), pp. 71, 80, 82.

4. Zeichner, "Transition," *Agricultural History*, p. 25. (See also fn. 2.)

5. James Larry Roark, "Masters Without Slaves: Southern Planters in the Civil War and Reconstruction" (unpublished doctoral dissertation, Stanford University, 197), p. 229.

6. The following two paragraphs are based on Roger Wallace Shugg, "Survival of the Plantation System in Louisiana," *Journal of Southern History*, (August 1937); Rowland T. Berthoff, "Southern Attitudes toward Immigration 1865–1914," *Journal of Southern History* (August 1951); Bert James Loewenberg, "Efforts of the South to Encourage Immigration 1865–1900," *South Atlantic Quarterly* (October 1934).

7. Shugg, "Survival," p. 321. (See also fn. 6.)

8. Zeichner, "Transition," pp. 25-26. (See also fn. 2.)

9. Robert Preston Brooks, "The Agrarian Revolution in Georgia 1865–1912," Bulletin of the University of Wisconsin, No. 639 (Madison: The University of Wisconsin, 1914), pp. 25-47.

10. For more on the question of landlord supervision with share arrangements, see Chapter IV.

11. Pete Daniel, *The Shadow of Slavery, Peonage in the South 1901–1969* (New York: Oxford University Press, 1973), p. 11.

12. This estimate is offered in George W. Groh, *The Black Migration: The Journey to Urban America* (New York: Weybright and Talley, 1972), p. 37, but is unsubstantiated. A WPA survey in 1933 revealed that for black sharecroppers the average length of residence per farm was 5.6 years. See T. J. Woofter, et al., *Landlord and Tenant on the Cotton Plantation*, Research Monograph 5, Division of Social Research, Works Progress Administration (Washington: Government Printing Office, 1936), p. 110.

13. Groh, *The Black Migration*, pp. 36-37. (See fn. 12.)

14. U. S. Census, 1890, Vol. 1, Part 2, Table 77; U. S. Census, 1910, Vol. 4, Table 10.

15. Brinley Thomas, *Migration and Economic Growth*, 2nd ed. (Cambridge: Cambridge University Press, 1973), p. 330.

16. See Robert Higgs, "Race, Skills, and Earnings: American Immigrants in 1909," *The Journal of Economic History*, 31, (June 1971); and *The Transformation of the American Economy 1865–1915* (New York: Wiley, 1971), pp. 115-22.

17. Oscar Zeichner, "The Legal Status of the Agricultural Laborer in the South," *Political Science Quarterly*, 55:3 (September 1940), p. 426.

18. *Ibid.*, p. 428.

19. Joseph D. Reid, "Sharecropping as an Understandable Market Response: The Postbellum South," *The Journal of Economic History* 33:1 (March 1973); Steven N. S. Cheung, *The Theory of Share Tenancy* (Chicago: University of Chicago Press, 1969). See also Robert Higgs, "Race, Tenure and Resource Allocation in Southern Agriculture, 1910," *The Journal of Economic History* 33:1 (March 1973); Robert Higgs, "Patterns of Farm Rental in the Georgia Cotton Belt, 1880-1900," *The Journal of Economic History* 34:2 (June 1974).

20. Stephen J. DeCanio, *Agriculture in the Post-bellum South, 1880–1900* (Cambridge: The MIT Press, 1974), pp. 165-70.

III. THE CULTURE OF PATERNALISM

1. Eugene D. Genovese, *Roll, Jordan, Roll: The World the Slaves Made* (New York: Pantheon, 1974), pp. 3-7.

2. Gunnar Myrdal, *An American Dilemma, The Negro Problem and Modern Democracy* (New York: Harper and Brothers, 1944), pp. 459, 593.

3. Arthur F. Raper, *Preface to Peasantry, A Tale of Two Blackbelt Counties* (Chapel Hill: The University of North Carolina Press, 1936), p. 122.

4. W. T. Couch, "The Negro in the South," in W. T. Couch, ed., *Culture in the South* (Chapel Hill: The University of North Carolina Press, 1935), p. 451.

5. Genovese, *Roll, Jordan, Roll*, p. 111. (See also fn. 1.)

6. Cited in James Larry Roark, "Masters without Slaves: Southern Planters in the Civil War and Reconstruction," (unpublished doctoral dissertation, Stanford University, 1973), p. 323.

7. *Ibid.*, pp. 321, 327.

8. Allison Davis, Burleigh B. Gardner, and Mary R. Gardner, *Deep South: A Social and Anthropological Study of Caste and Class* (Chicago: University of Chicago Press, 1941), as quoted in George Groh, *The Black Migration: The Journey to Urban America* (New York: Weybright and Talley, 1972), pp. 43-44.

9. See C. Van Woodward, *The Strange Career of Jim Crow*, 3rd rev. ed. (New York: Oxford University Press, 1974).

10. James Elbert Cutler, *Lynch-Law, an Investigation into the History of Lynching in the United States* (orig. ed. 1905 reprinted, Montclair: Patterson Smith, 1969), p. 179.

11. William H. Nicholls, *Southern Traditions and Regional Progress* (Chapel Hill: The University of North Carolina Press, 1960), pp. 54-55.

12. C. Van Woodward, *Origins of the New South 1877–1913* (Baton Rouge: Louisiana State University Press, 1951), pp. 107-28.

13. Quoted in Groh, *The Black Migration*, p. 5. (See also fn. 8.)

14. Richard A. Easterlin, "The American Population," in Lance E. Davis et al., *American Economic Growth, An Economist's History of the United States* (New York: Harper and Row, 1972), p. 150.

15. Peter J. Hill has shown that before World War I, those blacks who were in the North occupied a lower occupational status relative to foreign born whites in the industrial labor force. Peter J. Hill, "Relative Skill and Income Levels of Native and Foreign Born Workers in the United States," *Explorations in Economic History 12*:1 (January 1975), pp. 58-59.

IV. TENANT PLANTATIONS IN THE POST-BELLUM SOUTH

1. U. S. Department of Commerce, Bureau of the Census, *Plantation Farming in the United States* (Washington: Government Printing Office, 1916).

2. *Ibid.*, p. 16.

3. *Ibid.*, p. 13.

4. *Ibid.*, Tables 11 and 12 were the sources for these calculations.

5. See Appendix 1 for the entire listing of plantation counties. We excluded plantation counties in the states of Florida, Tennessee, Texas, and Virginia. In these states plantation counties represented less than 20 percent of the states' counties. By excluding them, we were able also to omit large numbers of nonplantation counties in these states and thus avoid creating a substantial numerical discrepancy in our listings.

6. C. O. Brannen, *Relation of Land Tenure to Plantation Organization*, U. S. Department of Agriculture, Department Bulletin No. 1269 (October 1924), p. 2.

7. *Ibid.*, p. 42.

8. *Ibid.*, pp. 2 , 25.

9. Charles S. Johnson, Edwin R. Embree, and W. W. Alexander, *The Collapse of Cotton Tenancy, Summary of Field Studies and Statistical Surveys 1933–35* (Chapel Hill: The University of North Carolina Press, 1935), pp. 6, 7.

10. Brannen, *Relation of Land Tenure*, p. 32. (See also fn. 6.)

11. *Ibid.*, p. 42.

12. Morton Rubin, *Plantation County* (Chapel Hill: The University of North Carolina Press, 1951), pp. 10, 27.

13. Brannen, *Relation of Land Tenure*, pp. 42-43. (See also fn. 6.)

14. Donald Crichton Alexander, *The Arkansas Plantation, 1920–1942* (New Haven: Yale University Press, 1943), pp. 66-67.

15. H. H. Wooten, *Credit Problems of North Carolina Cropper Farmers*, North Carolina Agricultural Experiment Station, Bulletin 271 (May 1930) cited in T. J. Woofter et al., *Landlord and Tenant on the Cotton Plantation*, Research Monograph 5 (Washington: The Division of Social Research, Works Progress Administration, 1936), pp. 61-62.

16. Woofter et al., *Landlord and Tenant*, pp. 61-63. (See also fn. 15.)

17. Johnson, Embree, and Alexander, *The Collapse of Cotton Tenancy*, p. 9. (See also fn. 9.)

V. TECHNOLOGICAL CHANGE AND DEVELOPMENT

1. Simon Kuznets, "Modern Economic Growth: Findings and Reflections," in Simon Kuznets, *Population, Capital and Growth, Selected Essays* (New York: W. W. Norton and Company, 1973), p. 165. Emphasis in original.

2. Robert Freedman, ed., *Marx on Economics* (New York: Harcourt, Brace and Company, 1961), p. 15.

3. During these years the South as a whole grew about as rapidly as the rest of the country, with Easterlin estimating its relative per capita income at 51.0 percent of the rest of the country in both 1880 and 1900. See Richard A. Easterlin, "Regional Income Trends, 1840–1950," in Robert W. Fogel and Stanley L. Engerman, eds., *The Reinterpretation of American Economic History* (New York: Harper & Row, 1971), p. 40.

4. Nathan Rosenberg, "Science, Invention and Economic Growth," *The Economic Journal*, 84:3 3 (March 1974), p. 107.

5. James H. Street, *The New Revolution in the Cotton Economy, Mechanization and its Consequences* (Chapel Hill: The University of North Carolina Press, 1957), pp. 100-103.

6. *Ibid.*, p. 118.

7. William M. Parker, "Agriculture," in Lance Davis et al., *American Economic Growth, An Economist's History of the United States* (New York: Harper and Row, 1972), p. 385.

8. Jacob Schmookler, *Invention and Economic Growth* (Cambridge: Harvard University Press, 1966), p. 206.

9. Nathan Rosenberg, "The Direction of Technological Change: Inducement Mechanisms and Focusing Devices," *Economic Development and Cultural Change*, 18:1 (October 1969), pp. 1-24.

10. Lance E. Davis, "The Investment Market, 1870–1914: The Evolution of a National Market," *The Journal of Economic History*, 25:3 (September 1965), pp. 388-392.

11. Evidence that lower levels of investment occurred in cotton than in corn or wheat is contained in data on capital investment per acre by product compiled in the 1900 census. In that census year capital per acre in corn stood at $7.91; in wheat, $7.93; and in cotton, $4.78. See U.S. Department of Commerce, Bureau of the Census, *Historical Statistics of the United States*.

VI. MIGRATION NORTH

1. The phrase is used by Eugene D. Genovese in his "American Slaves and Their History," in Eugene D. Genovese, *In Red and Black: Marxian Explorations in Southern and Afro-American History* (New York: Vintage Books, 1971), p. 109.

2. Edward F. Denison, *Accounting for United States Economic Growth, 1929–1969* (Washington: The Brookings Institution, 1974), pp. 62-64.

3. Reynolds Farley, *Growth of the Black Population* (Chicago: Markham Publishing Company, 1971), pp. 46-47. Not infrequently, migrating blacks were recruited to the North to act as strikebreakers in a period of rising union militancy. See Ray Marshall, *The Negro and Organized Labor* (New York: Wiley, 1965), pp. 16-20.

4. Richard A. Easterlin, "The American Population," in Lance E. Davis et al., *American Economic Growth: An Economist's History of the United States* (New York: Harper and Row, 1972), p. 137.

5. *Historical Statistics of the United States*, Series C25-73. (See also fn. 11, Chapter V.)

6. Karl E. Taeuber and Alma F. Taeuber, "The Negro Population in the United States," in John P. Davis, ed., *The American Negro Reference Book* (Englewood Cliffs: Prentice-Hall, Inc., 1969), pp. 112-113.

7. T. J. Woofter noted just such changes as early as 1916–1917. See his *Negro Migration, Changes in Rural Organization and Population of the Cotton Belt* (New York: AMS, 1971, first published 1920), pp. 156-157.

8. Taeuber and Taeuber, "The Negro Population," pp. 112-113. (See also fn. 6.)

9. The relief statistics are taken from Raymond Walters, *Negroes and the Great Depression, The Problem of Economic Recovery* (Westport: Greenwood Publishing Corporation, 1970), p. 91 and Mary Ellison, *The Black Experience: American Blacks since 1865* (New York: Barnes and Noble, 1974), p. 123.

10. Arnold Rose, *The Negro in America* (New York: Harper and Brothers, 1948), pp. 120-121.

11. The following two paragraphs are based on and quotations taken from David Eugene Conrad, *The Forgotten Farmers, The Story of Sharecroppers in the New Deal* (Urbana: University of Illinois Press, 1965), pp. 43-44.

12. *Ibid.*, p. 76.

13. Gunnar Myrdal, *An America Dilemma, The Negro Problem and Modern Democracy* (New York: Harper and Brothers, 1944), p. 253.

14. Ellison, *Black Experience*, pp. 114-115. (See also fn. 9.)

15. Theodore Rosengarten, *All God's Dangers: The Life of Nate Shaw* (New York: Alfred A. Knopf, 1974), pp. 296-309.

VII. BREAKDOWN OF THE PLANTATION ECONOMY

1. "War and Post-War Trends in Employment of Negroes," *Monthly Labor Review* (January 1945), p. 4.

2. Robert C. Weaver, *Negro Labor, A National Problem* (New York: Harcourt, Brace and Company, 1946), p. 27.

3. Abram J. Jaffe and Seymour L. Wolfbein, "Post-War Migration Plans of Army Enlisted Men," *The Annals 238* (March 1945).

4. "War and Post-War Trends," p. 5. (See also fn. 1.)

5. James H. Street, *The New Revolution in the Cotton Economy, Mechanization and its Consequences* (Chapel Hill: The University of North Carolina Press, 1957), p. 193.

6. U. S. Department of Labor, *Crops and Markets* (January 1946), p. 45.

7. Seymour Melman, "An Industrial Revolution in the Cotton South," *Economic History Review* (1949), p. 64.

8. *Ibid.*, p. 64.

9. Street, *New Revolution*, pp. 129-130. (See also fn. 5.)

10. *Ibid.*, p. 130.

11. Richard H. Day, "The Economics of Technological Change and the Demise of the Sharecropper," *The American Economic Review*, 57:3 (June 1967), pp. 429-430.

12. *Ibid.*, p. 436.

13. *Ibid.*, p. 439.

VIII. POST-PLANTATION BLACK EXPERIENCE

1. *Historical Statistics of the United States, Colonial Times to 1970*, Bicentennial Edition, Series C25-75 (Washington: Government Printing Office, 1975).
2. U.S. Bureau of the Census, *Census of Population 1970*, Vol. 1, *Characteristics of the Population*, Parts 2,5. 12, 20, 26, and 42 (Washington: Government Printing Office, 1973).
3. Data in the following two paragraphs are computed from Sar A. Levitan, William B. Johnston and Robert Taggert, *Still a Dream, The Changing Status of Blacks Since 1960* (Cambridge: Harvard University Press, 1975), pp. 28-31.
4. *Ibid.*, p. 46.

IX. STRATEGIES OF CHANGE

1. Vernon Wharton, *The Negro in Mississippi, 1865–1890* (Chapel Hill: The University of North Carolina Press, 1947), p. 59.
2. August Meier, *Negro Thought in America, 1880–1915* (Ann Arbor: The University of Michigan Press, 1963). p. 44.
3. *Ibid.*, p. 104.
4. *Ibid.*, p. 105.
5. W. E. B. Du Bois, *The Souls of Black Folk, Essays and Sketches* (Chicago: A. C. McClurg and Company, 1903), p. 38.
6. *Ibid.*, p. 52.
7. *Ibid.*, p. 52.
8. See, for example, Harold Cruse, "Revolutionary Nationalism and the Afro-American," in James Weinstein and David W. Eakins, eds., *For A New America, Essays in History and Politics from Studies on the Left, 1959–1967* (New York: Random House, 1970), pp. 355-356.
9. Meier, *Negro Thought in America*, p. 106. (See also fn. 2.)
10. Quoted in Roi Ottley, *The Lonely Warrior, The Life and Times of Robert S. Abbott* (Chicago: Henry Regnery Company, 1955), p. 160.
11. Florette Henri, *Black Migration Movement North 1900–1920* (Garden City: Anchor Press/Doubleday, 1975), p. 64.
12. Ottley, *The Lonely Warrior*, p. 167. (See also fn. 10.)
13. Amy Jacques-Garvey, ed., *Philosophy and Opinions of Marcus Garvey* (New York: Atheneum, 1969) 1, p. 38.
14. Cruse, "Revolutionary Nationalism and the Afro-American," p. 357. (See also fn. 8.)
15. Elton C. Fax, *Garvey, The Story of a Pioneer Black Nationalist* (New York: Dodd, Mead and Company, 1972), pp. 145-146.
16. Jacques-Garvey, *Philosophy and Opinions*, 1, p. 39. (See also fn. 13.)
17. Robert L. Allen, *Black Awakening in Capitalist America: An Analytic History* (Garden City: Doubleday and Company, Inc., 1970), p. 102.
18. William Z. Foster, *The Negro People in American History* (New York: International Publishers Company, 1954), p. 461.
19. James S. Allen, *The Negro Question in the United States* (New York: International Publishers, 1936).
20. Robert L. Allen, *Black Awakening*, p. 102. (See also fn. 17.)

X. CURRENT PROSPECTS

1. Mary Ellison, *The Black Experience: American Blacks Since 1865* (New York: Barnes and Noble, 1974), p.183.
2. James Tobin, "On Improving the Economic Status of the Negro," in William G. Bowen and Orley Ashenfelter, eds., *Labor and the National Economy* (New York: W. W. Norton and Company, 1975), p. 69.

SELECTED BIBLIOGRAPHY

Alexander, David C. *The Arkansas Plantation 1920–1942.* New Haven: Yale University Press, 1943.

Allen, James S. *The Negro Question in the United States.* New York: International Publishers, 1936.

Allen, Robert L. *Black Awakening in Capitalist America: An Analytic History.* Garden City: Doubleday and Company, 1970.

Baldwin, Robert E. "Patterns of Development in Newly Settled Regions." *The Manchester School of Economic and Social Studies* (May 1956).

Baron, Harold. "The Demand for Black Labor, Historical Notes on the Political Economy of Racism." *Radical America* 5:2 (March–April 1971).

Barrow, D. C. "A Georgia Plantation." *Scribner's Monthly* (April 1881).

Beale, Calvin L. "The Negro in American Agriculture." In John P. Davis, ed., *The American Negro Reference Book.* Englewood Cliffs: Printice-Hall, 1969.

Beale, Carlton. "The Black Belt of the Caribbean." *The American Mercury* XXIV(October 1931).

Beardwood, Robert. "Southern Roots of Urban Crisis." *Fortune* 78 (August 1968).

Becker, Joseph A. "Effects of the Boll Weevil upon Cotton Production in the United States." *International Cotton Bulletin* (June 1924).

Beckford, George L. *Persistent Poverty, Underdevelopment in Plantation Economies of the Third World.* New York, London, Toronto: Oxford University Press, 1972.

Bedell, M. S. "Employment and Income of Negro Workers, 1940–1952." *Monthly Labor Review* (June 1953).

Benns, Sir Bernard. "Plantation and Other Centrally Operated Estates." Rome, FAO, *Agricultural Studies* 28 (June 1955).

Bentley, George. *History of the Freedmen's Bureau.* Philadelphia: University of Pennsylvania Press, 1955.

Berthoff, Rowland T. "Southern Attitudes Toward Immigration 1865–1914." *The Journal of Southern History* XVII:3 (August 1951).

Brannen, C. O. "Limitations of the Plantation System as a Basis for Progress of the Tenants." *Southwestern Social Science Quarterly* (December 1949).

Brooks, Robert P. *The Agrarian Revolution in Georgia 1865–1912.* Madison: University of Wisconsin, 1914.

Cheung, S. N. S. *The Theory of Share Tenancy.* Chicago: University of Chicago Press, 1969.

Clark, Thomas D. "The Furnishing and Supply System in Southern Agriculture Since 1865." *Journal of Southern History* XII:1 (February 1946).

Coe, Paul. "The Nonwhite Population Surge to Our Cities." *Land Economics* 35 (August 1959).

Conrad, David E. *The Forgotten Farmers: The Story of Sharecroppers in the New Deal.* Urbana: University of Illinois Press, 1965.

Cooper, Martin R., Glen T. Barton, and Albert P. Brodell. *Progress of Farm Mechanization.* U. S. Department of Agriculture Miscellaneous Publication No. 630.

Cooper, William J. *The Conservative Regime: South Carolina, 1877–1890.* Baltimore: The Johns Hopkins Press, 1968.

Couch, W. T. *Culture in the South.* Chapel Hill: The University of North Carolina Press, 1935.

Cox, Lawanda. "Agricultural Labor in the United States, 1865–1900, with Special Reference to the South." Unpublished doctoral thesis. University of California, 1941.

————. "The Promise of Land for the Freedman." *Mississippi Valley Historical Review* XLV (1958).

Cox, Lawanda and John H. Cox. *Politics, Principles and Prejudice: 1865–1866.* New York: Free Press of Glencoe, Macmillan, 1967.

Cruse, Harold. "Revolutionary Nationalism and the Afro-American." In James Weinstein and David Eakins, eds., *For A New America: Essays in History and Politics from Studies of the Left 1959–1967.* New York: Random House, 1970.

Cutler, James E. *Lynch Law: An Investigation into the History of Lynching in the United States.* Original edition 1905. Reprinted by Montclair: Patterson Smith, 1969.

Daniel, Pete. *The Shadow of Slavery, Peonage in the South, 1901–1969.* New York: Oxford University Press, 1973.

Davis, Allison, Burleigh B. Gardner, and Mary R. Gardner. *Deep South: A Social and Anthropological Study of Caste and Class.* Chicago: The University of Chicago Press, 1941.

Davis, Lance E. "The Investment Market 1870–1914: The Evolution of a National Market." *The Journal of Economic History* XXV:3 (September 1965).

Day, Richard H. "The Economics of Technological Change and the Demise of the Sharecropper." *American Economic Review* LVII:3 (June 1967).

DeCanio, Stephen. *Agriculture in the Postbellum South.* Cambridge: The MIT Press, 1974.

Denison, Edward F. *Accounting for United States Economic Growth 1929–1969.* Washington: The Brookings Institution, 1974.

Dillingham, Harry C. and David Sly. "Mechanical Cotton-Picker, Negro Migration and the Integration Movement." *Human Organization* 25 (Winter 1966).

Dobb, Maurice. *Studies in the Development of Capitalism.* New York: International Publishers, 1947.

————. "Transition from Feudalism to Capitalism." In Maurice Dobb, ed., *Papers on Capitalism Development and Planning.* New York: International Publishers, 1967.

Domar, Evsey D. "The Causes of Slavery or Serfdom: A Hypothesis." *The Journal of Economic History* XXX (1970).

Donald, Henderson H. *The Negro Freedman: Life Conditions of the American Negro in the Early Years after Emancipation.* New York: Henry Schuman, 1952.

Dowd, Douglas. "A Comparative Analysis of Economic Development in the American West and South." *The Journal of Economic History* XVI:4 (December 1956).

DuBois, W. E. B. "The Negro Farmer" in U. S. Bureau of the Census. *Special Reports,* Supplementary Analysis and Derivation Tables, 12th Census of the United States: 1900. Washington: Government Printing Office, 1906.

———. *The Souls of Black Folk, Essays and Sketches.* Chicago: A. C. McClury and Company, 1903.

Dunn, Richard S. *Sugar and Slaves: The Rise of the Planter Class in the English West Indies.* Chapel Hill: The University of North Carolina Press, 1972.

Easterlin, Richard A. "The American Population." In Lance E. Davis et al., *American Economic Growth, An Economist's History of the United States.* New York: Harper and Row, 1972.

———. "Influences in European Overseas Emigration before World War I." *Economic Development and Cultural Change* IX:3 (April 1961).

———. "Regional Income Trends 1840–1950." In Robert W. Fogel and Stanley Engerman, eds., *The Reinterpretation of American Economic History.* New York: Harper and Row, 1971.

Ellison, Mary. *The Black Experience: American Blacks Since 1865.* New York: Barnes and Noble, 1974.

Engerman, Stanley. "Some Considerations Relating to Property Rights in Man." *The Journal of Economic History* XXXIII:1 (March 1973).

———. "Some Economic Factors in Southern Backwardness in the Nineteenth Century." In John F. Kain and John R. Meyers, eds., *Essays in Regional Economics.* Cambridge: Harvard University Press, 1971.

Evans, Robert, Jr. "Some Notes on Coerced Labor." *The Journal of Economic History* XXX:1 (1970).

Farley, Reynolds. *Growth of the Black Population: A Study of Demographic Trends.* Chicago: Markham Publishing Company, 1970.

Fax, Elton C. *Garvey, The Story of a Pioneer Black Nationalist.* New York: Dodd, Mead and Company, 1972.

Fite, Gilbert C. "Recent Progress in the Mechanization of Cotton Production in the United States." *Agricultural History* 24 (January 1950).

Foster, William Z. *The Negro People in American History.* New York: International Publishers, 1954.

Frank, A. G., *Capitalism and Underdevelopment in Latin America.* New York: Monthly Review Press, 1967.

Freedman, Robert, ed. *Marx on Economics.* New York: Harcourt Brace, 1961.

Garvey, Amy Jacques, ed. *Philosophy and Opinions of Marcus Garvey.* New York: Atheneum, 1969.

Genovese, Eugene D. *In Red and Black: Marxian Explorations in Southern and Afro-American History*. New York: Vintage Books, 1971.

———. *Roll, Jordan, Roll: The World the Slaves Made*. New York: Pantheon, 1974.

———. *The World the Slaveholders Made*. New York: Vintage Books, 1971.

Glenn, Norval D. "Some Changes in the Relative Status of American Nonwhites 1940 to 1960." *Phylon*, Second Quarter (1963).

Goldon, Claudia Dale. "The Economics of Emancipation." *Journal of Economic History* XXXIII:1 (March 1973).

Good, Park. *The American Serfs*. New York: G. P. Putnam and Sons, 1968.

Greene, Lorenzo J. and Carter G. Woodson. *The Negro Wage Earner*. Washington: The Association for the Study of Negro Life and History, Inc., 1930.

Groh, George W. *The Black Migration: The Journey to Urban America*. New York: Weybright and Talley, 1972.

Hamilton, C. Horace. "Educational Selectivity of Net Migration from the South." *Social Forces* 38 (October 1959).

———. "The Negro Leaves the South." *Demography* 1 (1964).

Hayami, Yugiro and Vernon W. Rutton. *Agricultural Development: An International Perspective*. Baltimore: The Johns Hopkins Press, 1971.

———. "Professor Rosenberg and the Direction of Technological Change: A Comment." *Economic Development and Cultural Change* 21:2 (January 1973).

Heer, Clarence. *Income and Wages in the South*. Chapel Hill: The University of North Carolina Press, 1930.

Henri, Florette. *Black Migration Movement North 1900–1920*. Garden City: Anchor Press/Doubleday, 1975.

Hiestand, Dale. *Economic Growth and Employment Opportunities for Minorities*. New York: Columbia University Press, 1964.

Higgs, Robert. "The Boll Weevil, The Cotton Economy and Black Migration 1910–1930." *Agricultural History* 50:2 (April 1976).

———. "Did Southern Farmers Discriminate?" *Agricultural History* 46 (April 1972).

———. "Patterns of Farm Rental in the Georgia Cotton Belt, 1880–1900." *The Journal of Economic History* XXXIV:2 (June 1974).

———. "Race, Skills and Earnings: American Immigrants in 1909." *The Journal of Economic History* XXXI:2 (June 1971).

———. "Race Tenure and Resource Allocation in Southern Agriculture." *The Journal of Economic History* XXXIII:1 (March 1973).

———. *The Transformation of the American Economy*. New York: Wiley, 1971.

Hill, Peter J. "Relative Skill and Income Levels of Native and Foreign Born Workers in the United States." *Explorations in Economic History* 12:1 (January 1975).

Historical Statistics of the United States, Colonial Times to 1971. Washington: Government Printing Office, 1975.

Historical Statistics of the United States, Colonial Times to 1957. Washington: Government Printing Office, 1960.

Hoover, Calvin B. and B. U. Ratchford. *Economic Resources and Policies of the South.* New York: Macmillan, 1951.

Jaffe, Abram and Seymour L. Wolfbein. "Postwar Migration Plans of Army Enlisted Men." *The Annals* 238 (March 1945).

Johnson, Alvin S. "Capitalism of the Camp." *The New Republic* VI (April 1, 1916).

Johnson, Charles. *Statistical Atlas of Southern Counties.* Chapel Hill: The University of North Carolina Press, 1941.

Johnson, Charles, Edwin R. Embee, and W. W. Alexander. *The Collapse of Cotton-Tenancy—Summary of Field Studies and Statistical Surveys, 1933–35.* Chapel Hill: The University of North Carolina Press, 1935.

Johnson, D. Gale. "Resource Allocation Under Share Contracts." *Journal of Political Economy* LVIII (April 1950).

———. "Southern Paternalism towards Negroes after Emancipation." *Journal of Southern History* XXIII (November 1957).

Jones, William O. "Plantations." In *The International Encyclopedia of the Social Science*, David Sills, ed., 12.

Kelsey, Carl. *The Negro Farmer.* Chicago: Jennings and Pye, 1903.

Kolchen, Peter. *First Freedom.* Westport: Greenways Press, 1972.

Kuznets, Simon. *Population, Capital and Growth: Selected Essays.* New York: W. W. Norton, 1973.

Lacy, Dan. *The White Use of Blacks in America.* New York: McGraw-Hill, 1972.

Land, Aubrey C., ed. *Basis of the Plantation Society.* Columbia: University of South Carolina Press, 1969.

Lander, Ernest M. *A History of South Carolina 1865–1960.* 2nd ed. Columbia: University of South Carolina Press, 1970.

Lebergott, Stanley. *Manpower in Economic Growth: The American Record since 1800.* New York: McGraw-Hill, 1964.

Lerner, Eugene. "Southern Output and Income 1860–1880." *Journal of Agricultural History* 33:3 (July 1959).

Levitan, Sar A., William B. Johnston, and Robert Taggert. *Still A Dream: The Changing Status of Blacks Since 1960.* Cambridge: Harvard University Press, 1975.

Loewenberg, Bert J. "Efforts of the South to Encourage Immigration, 1865–1900." *The South Atlantic Quarterly* (October 1934).

Logan, F. A. *The Negro in North Carolina 1876–1894.* Chapel Hill: University of North Carolina Press, 1964.

Mandle, Jay R. "The Plantation Economy: An Essay in Definition." *Science and Society* XXXVI (Spring 1972).

———. "The Plantation Economy and Its Aftermath." *Review of Radical Political Economics* 6:1 (Spring 1974).

————. *The Plantation Economy: Population and Economic Change in Guyana 1838–1960*. Philadelphia: Temple University Press, 1973.

————. "The Plantation States as a Subregion of the Post-Bellum South." *The Journal of Economic History* XXIV:3 (September 1974).

————. "The Re-establishment of the Plantation Economy in the South, 1865–1910." *Review of Black Political Economy* 3:2 (Winter 1973).

Marshall, Ray. *The Negro and Organized Labor*. New York: Wiley, 1965.

McFeeley, William S. *Yankee Stepfather: General O. O. Howard and the Freedmen*. New Haven and London: Yale University Press, 1968.

Meier, August. *Negro Thought in America 1880–1915*. Ann Arbor: The University of Michigan Press, 1963.

Melman, Seymour. "An Industrial Revolution in the Cotton South." *Economic History Review* (1949).

Mintz, S. W. "Toward an Afro-american History." *Journal of World History* 13 (1971).

Myint, Hla. *The Economics of Developing Countries*. New York: Praeger, 1969.

Myrdal, Gunnar. *An American Dilemma: The Negro Problem and Modern Democracy*. New York: Harper, 1944.

Neal, Ernest, and Lewis Jones. "The Place of the Negro Farmer in the Changing Economy of the Cotton South." *Rural Sociology* 15 (March 1950).

Nicholls, William H. "Multiple-Unit Operations and Gross Farm Income Distribution within the Old Cotton Belt." *Southern Economics Journal* XIX (1953).

————. *Southern Traditions and Regional Progress*. Chapel Hill: The University of North Carolina Press, 1960.

Ottley, Roi. *The Lonely Warrior: The Life and Times of Robert S. Abbott*. Chicago: Henry Regnery Company, 1955.

Parker, William M. "Agriculture." In Lance Davis et al., *American Economic Growth, An Economist's History of the United States*. New York: Harper and Row, 1973.

Pederson, H. A. "Mechanized Agriculture and the Farm Laborer." *Rural Sociology* 19 (June 1954).

Phillips, U.B. "The Decadence of the Plantation System." *The Annals of the American Academy of Political and Social Science* XXXV (January 1910).

————. "The Plantation with Slave Labor and Free." *American Historical Review* CCXIX (July 1925).

Pruntz, Merle. "The Renaissance of the Southern Plantation." *The Geographic Review* (October 1955).

Raper, Arthur F. *Preface to Peasantry*. Chapel Hill: University of North Carolina Press, 1936.

Reid, Joseph D. "Sharecropping as an Understandable Market Response—The Post-Bellum South." *The Journal of Economic History* XXXIII:1 (March 1973).

Roark, James L. "Masters Without Slaves: Southern Plantations in the Civil War and Reconstruction." Unpublished doctoral dissertation. Stanford University, 1973.

Roback, Herbert. "Legal Barriers to Interstate Migration." *Cornell Law Quarterly* 28:3 and 4.

Rose, Arnold. *The Negro in America.* New York: Harper and Brothers, 1948.

Rosenberg, Nathan. "The Direction of Technological Change: Inducement Mechanisms and Focusing Devices." *Economic Development and Cultural Change* 18:1 (October 1969).

———. "Science, Invention and Economic Growth." *The Economic Journal* 84:333 (March 1974).

———. "The Direction of Technological Change: A Reply." *Economic Development and Cultural Change* 21:2 (January 1973).

Rosengarten, Theodore. *All God's Dangers: The Life of Nate Shaw.* New York: Alfred A. Knopf, 1974.

Rubin, Morton. *Plantation County.* Chapel Hill: The University of North Carolina Press, 1951.

Saloutor, Theodore. "Southern Agriculture and the Problems of Readjustment." *Agricultural History* 30:1 (January 1956).

Schmookler, Jacob. *Inventions and Economic Growth.* Cambridge: Harvard University Press, 1966.

———. *Patents, Inventions and Economic Change.* Data and selected essays edited by Zvi Griliches and Leonid Hurwicz. Cambridge: Harvard University Press, 1972.

Shugg, Roger W. "Survival of the Plantation System in Louisiana." *Journal of Southern History* (August 1937).

Street, James. *The New Revolution in the Cotton Economy.* Chapel Hill: The University of North Carolina Press, 1957.

———. "Mechanizing the Cotton Harvest." In the *Annual Report of the Smithsonian Institution*, 1957, Publication 4314. Washington: U. S. Government Printing Office, 1958.

Stone, Alfred H. "The Negro in the Yazoo-Mississippi Delta." *Proceedings of the American Economic Association, Dec. 27-30, 1901.* 3rd series, 3, 1902.

Sutch, Richard. "Discussion of Slavery and Economic Growth." *The Journal of Economic History* XXVII (December 1967).

Sutch, Richard, and Roger Ransom. "The Ex-Slaves in the Post-Bellum South: A Study of the Economic Impact of Racism in a Market Economy." *The Journal of Economic History* XXXIII:1 (March 1973).

Taeuber, Karl E. and Alma F. Taeuber. "The Negro Population in the United States." In John P. Davis, ed., *The American Negro Reference Book.* Englewood Cliffs: Prentice-Hall, 1966.

Tang, Anthony. *Economic Development in the South Piedmont 1860–1950.* Chapel Hill: The University of North Carolina Press, 1958.

Taylor, P. S. "Plantation Agriculture in the United States, Seventeenth to Twentieth Century." *Land Economics* (May 1954).

Thomas, Brinley. *Migration and Economic Growth*. 2nd ed. Cambridge: Cambridge University Press, 1973.

Thompson, Edgar. T. "The South in Old and New Concepts." In John T. McKinney and Edgar T. Thompson, eds., *The South in Continuity and Change.* Durham, N.C.: Duke University Press, 1965.

———. "The Natural History of Agricultural Labor in the South." In David P. Jackson, ed., *American Studies in Honor of William Kenneth Boyd*. Durham, N. C.: Duke University Press, 1940.

———. "The Plantation." Unpublished doctoral dissertation, University of Chicago, 1938.

———. "The Plantation: The Physical Basis of Traditional Race Relations." In Edgar T. Thompson, ed., *Race Relations and the Race Problem*. Durham, N. C.: Duke University Press, 1968 (Available from Greenwood Press, New York).

———. *Plantation Societies, Race Relations and the South: The Regimentation of Populations*. Durham, N.C.: Duke University Press, 1975.

———. "Population Expansion and the Plantation System." *American Journal of Sociology* XLI (November 1935).

Tobin, James. "On Improving the Economic Status of the Negro." In William G. Bowen and Orley Ashenfelter, eds., *Labor and the National Economy.* New York: W. W. Norton, 1975.

U. S. Bureau of the Census. Census of Population 1970, Vol. 1. *Characteristics of the Population*. Washington: Government Printing Office, 1973.

———. 13th Census of the U. S. 1910, Vol. 5, *Agriculture, General Report and Analysis*. Washington: Government Printing Office, 1913.

———. 13th Census of the U. S. 1910, Vols. 6, 7, *Agriculture, Report of States.* Washington: Government Printing Office, 1912, 1913.

———. *Negro Population 1790–1915*. Washington: Government Printing Office, 1918.

———. *Plantation Farming in the United States*. Washington: Government Printing Office, 1916.

U. S. Dept. of Agriculture, Bureau of Agricultural Statistics. *Statistical Bulletin No. 99, Statistics on Cotton and Related Data*. Washington: Government Printing Office, June 1951.

———. Technical Bulletin No. 682. E. L. Langsford and B. M. Thebodeaus. *Plantation Organization and Operation in Yazoo-Mississippi Delta Area.* Washington: Government Printing Office, 1903.

U. S. Department of Labor. *Crops and Markets*. January 1946.

Vance, Rupert. *Human Factors in Cotton Culture*. Chapel Hill: University of North Carolina Press, 1937.

———. *Human Geography of the South*. 2nd ed. New York: Russell and Russell, 1968.

Wagley, Charles. "Plantation America: A Culture Sphere." In Vera Rubin, ed., *Caribbean Studies: A Symposium*. Seattle: University of Washington, 1960.

Wallerstein, Immanuel. *The Modern World System: Capitalist Agriculture and* the Origins of the European-World Economy in the Sixteenth Century. New York: Academic Press, 1974.

"War and Postwar Trends in Employment of Negroes." Monthly Labor Review (January 1945).

Weaver, Robert C. Negro Labor, A National Problem. New York: Harcourt Brace, 1946.

Wharton, Vernon L. The Negro in Mississippi 1865–1900. Chapel Hill: The University of North Carolina Press, 1947.

Williamson, Joel. After Slavery, The Negro in South Carolina during Reconstruction 1861–1877. Chapel Hill: The University of North Carolina Press, 1965.

Wolfbein, S. L. "War and Post-War Trends in Employment of Negroes." Monthly Labor Review, (January 1945).

Walters, Raymond. Negroes and the Great Depression: The Problem of Economic Recovery. Westport: Greenwood Publishing Company, 1970.

Woodman, Harold. King Cotton and His Retainers. Lexington: University of Kentucky Press, 1968.

Woodson, Carter G. The Rural Negro. New York: Russell and Russell, 1930.

Woodward, C. Van. Origins of the New South 1877–1913. Baton Rouge: Louisiana State University Press, 1951.

————. The Burden of Southern History. Baton Rouge: Louisiana State University Press, 1968.

Woody, Robert H. "The Labor and Immigrant Problem of South Carolina during Reconstruction." Mississippi Valley Historical Review XVIII (1931–1932).

Woofter, Thomas J. Negro Migration. Originally published 1920. New York: AMS, 1971.

Woofter, Thomas J., et al. Landlord and Tenant on the Cotton Plantation. Research Monograph V. Washington: Division of Social Research, Works Progress Administration, 1936.

Wright, Richard and Edwin Rosakam. 12 Million Black Voices, A Folk History of the Negro in the United States. New York: The Viking Press, 1941.

Zeichner, Oscar. "Legal Status of the Agricultural Laborer in the South." Political Science Quarterly (September 1940).

————. "The Transition from Slave to Free Agricultural Labor in the Southern States." Agricultural History XIII (June 1939).

INDEX